Master the MAT 2022

Master the MAT 2022

September 2, 2022

Copyright 2022 by Oxbridge Mind.

All rights reserved. No part of this publication may be reproduced, stored or transmitted in any form or by any means, electronic, mechanical, photocopying, recording, scanning, or otherwise without written permission from the publisher. It is illegal to copy this book, post it to a website, or distribute it by any other means without permission.

First edition.

Contents

1	**Introduction to the MAT**	**2**
	1.1 What is the MAT	2
	1.2 Preparation	7
2	**Strategies for problem solving**	**14**
	2.1 Where to begin	14
	2.2 Methods of Argument	16
	2.3 Walkthrough: MAT 2010 Question 6	22
3	**Algebra**	**26**
	3.1 Logarithm	26
	3.2 Solving Inequalities	28
	3.3 Bounding	31
	3.4 Walkthrough: MAT 2021 Question 2	32
	3.5 Common traps	36
4	**Geometry**	**38**
	4.1 Coordinate Geometry	38
	4.2 Lines and Vectors	40
	4.3 Walkthrough: MAT 2009 Question 4	45
	4.4 Circles	49
	4.5 Walkthrough: MAT 2015 Question 4	54
5	**Trigonometry**	**60**
	5.1 Definitions of Trigonometric Functions	60
	5.2 Basic Identities	61
	5.3 Plots of Trigonometric Functions	63
	5.4 Solving equations	65
	5.5 Walkthrough: MAT 2010 Question P3	66
6	**Functions and Polynomials**	**70**
	6.1 Functions	70

	6.2 Functional equations	72
	6.3 Walkthrough: MAT 2007 Question 2	73
	6.4 Polynomials	76
	6.5 Factorisation	80
	6.6 Walkthrough, Specimen B Question 2	84
	6.7 Common traps	86

7 Differentiation — 88
- 7.1 Definition — 88
- 7.2 Monotonicity — 91
- 7.3 Turning Points — 92
- 7.4 Walkthrough: MAT Specimen B Question 3 — 95
- 7.5 Common traps — 97

8 Integration — 100
- 8.1 Integration as area — 100
- 8.2 Trapezium Rule — 101
- 8.3 Indefinite Integration — 103
- 8.4 Walkthrough: MAT 2011 Question 3 — 104

9 Graph Transformation — 108
- 9.1 Plotting common functions — 108
- 9.2 Relation between $f(x)$ and $f'(x)$ — 113
- 9.3 Transformations — 117

10 Sequences and Series — 124
- 10.1 Arithmetic and Geometric Series — 124
- 10.2 Recursive sequences — 127
- 10.3 Walkthrough: MAT 2016 Question 5 — 129

11 Algorithms and Games — 134
- 11.1 Procedures — 134
- 11.2 Winning Games Mathematically — 137
- 11.3 Walkthrough: MAT 2018 Question 6 — 138
- 11.4 Walkthrough: MAT 2012 Question 7 — 140

12 Number Theory — 144
- 12.1 Divisibility — 144
- 12.2 Walkthrough: MAT 2015 Question 2 — 146

13 Combinatorics and Probability — 150
- 13.1 Combinatorics — 150
- 13.2 Probability — 153

13.3 Walkthrough: MAT 2010 Question 7 157

CHAPTER 1

Introduction to the MAT

1.1 What is the MAT

The Mathematics Admissions Test, known throughout as MAT, is one of the aptitude tests used for the admissions process in the University of Oxford, Imperial College London and the University of Warwick. The MAT is also taken into consideration by other universities in the UK, including Bath and Durham for particular courses.

It iss a 2-hour and 30-minute long written test on mathematics. Candidates take the MAT exam as part of their initial application to Oxford, Imperial or Warwick. The courses that require MAT as part of the application are as follows:

University of Oxford If you're applying for one of the following courses at the University of Oxford, you'll need to sit the MAT:

1. Mathematics
2. Mathematics and Statistics
3. Mathematics and Philosophy
4. Computer Science
5. Mathematics and Computer Science
6. Computer Science and Philosophy

The university then makes a shortlist of candidates based on their results in the MAT and their UCAS application and invites them for interviews. The interviews are the last stage of the admission process, after which the university send out their admission offers to successful candidates.

Imperial College London If you are applying for the following courses at the Imperial College London, it is required that you sit the MAT:

Mathematics Courses Three-year courses:

1. BSc Mathematics
2. BSc Mathematics with Applied Mathematics/Mathematical Physics
3. BSc Mathematics with Mathematical Computation
4. BSc Mathematics with Statistics
5. BSc Mathematics with Statistics for Finance

Four-year courses

1. MSci Mathematics
2. MSci Mathematics with a Year Abroad

Joint Mathematics and Computing courses Three-year course:

1. BEng Mathematics and Computer Science

Four-year course:

1. MEng Mathematics and Computer Science

University of Warwick If you are applying to any of the following courses at the University of Warwick, you will need to sit the MAT:

1. Mathematics BSc
2. Master of Mathematics

Additionally, the University of Bath and Durham University will have access to your MAT score. The MAT scores are automatically sent to these universities with encryption, preventing them from viewing your score without your permission. If you wish these universities to take your MAT score into consideration, you must provide them with your MAT registration number.

Your MAT score will be taken into consideration if you apply to the following courses at these universities:

Durham University Mathematics courses:

1. Mathematics BSc
2. Mathematics MMath
3. Mathematics and Statistics BSc
4. Mathematics and Statistics MMath

University of Bath Your MAT score will be considered for the following courses:

1. BSc Mathematics
2. MMath Mathematics
3. BSc Mathematical Sciences
4. BSc Mathematics & Statistics
5. BSc Computer Science & Mathematics
6. MComp Computer Science & Mathematics
7. BSc Economics & Mathematics

The details of this information can be found on the website of the Department of Mathematics of the University of Oxford in the following link:
https://www.maths.ox.ac.uk/study-here/undergraduate-study/maths-admissions-test

Format of MAT

The MAT is a 2 hours and 30 minutes written test taken at official authorised test centres all over the world. The test has two sections - The first is a multiple-choice answer-based section, and the second a proof-based section.

Question 1: Multiple-choice questions

In this section, there are 10 multiple-choice questions, each worth 4 points. Marks are given solely for the correct answers, though students are encouraged to show any working out. The questions themselves range over all the topics in the MAT syllabus which we will discuss shortly. **Every candidate must attempt this section.**

Question 2-7: Proof-based questions

In this section, each candidate must attempt 4 proof-based questions from 6 choices depending on the courses for which they are applying. Each question is divided into smaller parts which usually are arranged in increasing order of difficulty. Each question is worth a total of 15 points. If you did not arrive at the correct answer but still have some correct working, partial marks will be awarded.

Depending on the course for which the candidate is applying, they are required to attempt different questions. The details of which can be found below:

Oxford If you are applying to the University of Oxford, you have to attempt the following questions:

1. Mathematics, Mathematics and Philosophy, Mathematics and Statistics: *2, 3, 4, 5*

2. Mathematics and Computer Science: *2, 3, 5, 6*

3. Computer Science, Computer Science and Philosophy: *2, 5, 6, 7*

Imperial and Warwick If you are applying to any of the Mathematics and joint courses at the University of Warwick or Imperial College London, you should attempt the questions: *2, 3, 4, 5*

1.1. WHAT IS THE MAT

Syllabus of MAT

According to the CAAT website: "The MAT aims to test the depth of mathematical understanding of a student in the fourth term of their A-levels (or equivalent) rather than a breadth of knowledge. It is set with the aim of being approachable by all students, including those without Further Mathematics A-level, and those from other educational systems (e.g. Baccalaureate and Scottish Highers)."

As all of the candidates will be students of A-levels or equivalents, the universities want to make sure you are comfortable with all the topics in A level maths. That is why the MAT syllabus is based on the first year A level Maths, and a few topics from the fourth term of A level Maths. Below is the full list of topics on the syllabus for MAT:

- **Polynomials**: The quadratic formula. Completing the square. Discriminant. Factorisation. Factor Theorem.

- **Algebra**: Simple simultaneous equations in one or two variables. Solution of simple inequalities. Binomial Theorem with positive whole exponent. Combinations and binomial probabilities.

- **Differentiation**: Derivative of x^a, including for fractional exponents. Derivative of e^{kx}. Derivative of a sum of functions. Tangents and normals to graphs. Turning points. Second order derivatives. Maxima and minima. Increasing and decreasing functions. Differentiation from first principles.

- **Integration**: Indefinite integration as the reverse of differentiation. Definite integrals and the signed areas they represent. Integration of x^a (where $a \neq -1$) and sums thereof.

- **Graphs**: The graphs of quadratics and cubics. Graphs of
$$\sin x, \quad \cos x, \quad \tan x, \quad \sqrt{x}, \quad a^x, \quad \log_a x$$
Solving equations and inequalities with graphs.

- **Logarithms and powers**: Laws of logarithms and exponentials. Solution of the equation $a^x = b$.

- **Transformations**: The relations between the graphs
$$y = f(ax), \quad y = af(x), \quad y = f(x-a), \quad y = f(x) + a$$
and the graph of $y = f(x)$.

- **Geometry**: Co-ordinate geometry and vectors in the plane. The equations of straight lines and circles. Basic properties of circles. Lengths of arcs of circles.

- **Trigonometry**: Solution of simple trigonometric equations. The identities

$$\tan x = \frac{\sin x}{\cos x}, \quad \sin^2 x + \cos^2 x = 1, \quad \sin(90° - x) = \cos x.$$

Periodicity of sine, cosine and tangent. Sine and cosine rules for triangles.

- **Sequences and series**: Sequences defined iteratively and by formulae. Arithmetic and geometric progressions. Their sums. Convergence condition for infinite geometric progressions.

Besides the aforementioned topics, for computer science students it is useful to be familiar with the following topics:

- **Induction**: Weak induction, strong induction, proving with induction.

- **Graph Theory**: Definition of nodes/vertices, edges, paths, cycles. Theorems on trees and cycles. Graph algorithms like breath-first search, depth-first search etc.

- **Linear Recursions**: Solving systems of linear recursive sequences.

Where can I take the MAT?

You will sit the test in either your school or college or a local test centre. Any school or college can register to become a test centre, following the instructions on the following website:

http://www.admissionstesting.org/for-test-takers/mat/how-to-register/

Although your school has to register for the test, it is your responsibility to make sure your school knows that you should be sitting the MAT.

If your school or college cannot register to become a test centre, you will instead sit the test at a local test centre. You can use the following link to locate eligible test centres nearby:
http://www.admissionstesting.org/find-a-centre/

Important dates

Below are the important dates of the MAT 2022:

Date	Event
1 September 2022	Registration opens. Test centres can register candidates from this date
30 September 2022	Registration deadline
2 November 2022	Test date

Cost of the MAT

Cambridge Assessment Admissions Testing does not charge candidates who have applied to a course requiring the MAT at the University of Oxford.

Some centres charge an administration fee to candidates sitting the MAT which covers the cost of invigilation, despatch costs and room hire which are essential for running the test: contact your centre for details.

Can I retake the MAT?

There is only one MAT testing date per year, so you won't be able to retake the exam until next year. You take the MAT as part of your application to the universities, so if you do re-take the exam as part of your new application, your chosen universities won't know you've taken the test before.

1.2 Preparation

The MAT is very different from the secondary school exams that you've encountered until now. Getting yourself familiar with the topics and the test format is crucial for you to succeed in the test. In the following sections, we'll guide you through the significant steps of the preparation process for the MAT.

Before the exam

Preparing for the Journey

The first thing you need to do to start preparing for the MAT is to make sure you know all the topics on the MAT syllabus. Make sure you can comfortably answer all the questions on the following paper:

`https://www.maths.ox.ac.uk/system/files/attachments/mat_syllabus_practice.pdf`

If you are unclear about any of the topics, read more on it from textbooks, and practice more problems. In short, it is not a good idea to leave out any of the topics hoping they might not appear on the test. As the universities want to make sure you are comfortable with ALL of the topics on the syllabus, they will make sure to include at least one question on each topic. So get your pen and paper ready and start ticking off topics from the list as done.

Getting a taste of the MAT

So you are confident you know the syllabus by heart. Now it's time to try out some actual challenges. You can find all the past MAT papers and solutions in the following link.

`https://www.maths.ox.ac.uk/study-here/undergraduate-study/maths-admissions-test`

Open up a past paper from before 2009 - you don't want to use up the new papers just yet - and try out a few questions just to get a feel for the test. The past papers can easily be found online. It is better not to time these attempts, as at first you want to make sure you can solve the problems without any pressure. It's recommended that you attempt all the MCQ questions from the paper, as the questions will be from a large variety of topics, and attempting all of them will give you a better picture of the different types of questions that appear on the MAT.

Studying the solutions

As you practice with the past papers, go over the official solutions which can be found on the internet. Often the official solutions answer the questions in more efficient ways, so whether you succeeded in answering the question correctly or you got stuck at some point, there should be something new for you to learn from the official solutions. If you find some new technique in the solutions that you didn't know before, you should spend some time trying to include it into your arsenal.

Concise solution writing

Since the MAT is a written exam where you have to justify all your answers, you need to learn to write clear and concise solutions. This doesn't come naturally to most of us, and it takes practice. When you write proofs –

1. Focus on making your arguments clear to read.

1.2. PREPARATION

2. If there is any important point of your argument, mark it clearly. Use underlines and boxes to highlight important points.

3. Use a lot of space between your arguments so they don't become a huge jumble of words.

4. Figures and graphs not only help you solve the question, but also are very helpful to the readers of your proof.

5. If you aren't sure about any statement you're making, don't give wrong explanations. If you can't prove a statement, leave it unexplained. Do not write wrong maths, the tutors won't appreciate it.

It goes beyond saying that if your examiner doesn't understand your solution, you will not get the marks for it. Again, reviewing official solutions will be useful here. You should refer to the official solutions to learn their structure and the amount of rigor they expect from the students.

The following article is an excellent guide to writing better solutions:

`https://artofproblemsolving.com/blog/articles/how-to-write-a-solution`

Taking timed mock exams

After you've gained a fair amount of confidence with MAT style questions, you should see how you perform under exam conditions. You should take at least a couple of timed mock exams, where you sit for 2-hours and 30-minutes without distraction and try to simulate an actual exam. This will give you a better sense of how to utilise your time during the exam. After taking the first mock exam, you should spend some time asking yourself the following questions and finding answers to them-

1. Did I waste valuable time at any point in this exam? If so, how could I prevent this in future?

2. Did I get spend more time on a question than I should have?

3. Was there any type of question I particularly struggled with?

4. Should I allocate more time to this section/question than I am doing now?

This is why taking a few mock exams is helpful, as it will give you chances to test out different strategies, and learn from your mistakes.

Grading and setting expectations

After each mock exam, you must check the solutions and grade yourself and compare your score to the score distribution published by the universities. You might find your score to be inadequate in the first few mock exams. But that's okay. Firstly, you will improve over time. And secondly, you should keep in mind that the scores published are averages among the successful candidates. Which means, half of the successful candidates got below the average successful mark! This is quite easy to overlook when you compare yourself to those mean scores.

Also bear in mind that the MAT is only one element of the overall admission process. So if you get above average scores in the mock exams then amazing! But if you did not, don't get disheartened, keep practicing more, and try to improve where you lack, and your scores will hopefully improve as well.

Time management on problems

At this point of preparation, you probably have a solid understanding of your weaknesses and strengths. You probably know which questions are more time consuming, and which you can get correct fairly quickly. Now it is time for you to start strategising how you utilise your time during the actual exam. Obviously, there is no best way to take an exam. The strategy depends on you, which you should come up with yourself by trial-and-error. If you want to compare your strategy with that of someone else, then here's what I did in the MAT 2020. I applied for Mathematics and Computer Science, so I attempted the questions 1, 2, 3, 5, and 6.

1. I first glanced over all the questions I had to answer, and realised that I might need to spend more time on Q3 and Q5.

2. Then I began with Q1, as that's where I used to make a lot of calculation mistakes in my mock exams. I spent on average 5 minutes on the MCQ questions. I got stuck on a few of them, so instead of wasting time, I moved on, and left them for later.

3. Then I did Q2, did two parts on Q3, and I realised I didn't know how to solve the other parts. So I moved on to the next questions.

4. After solving both Q5 and Q6, I returned to Q3. This time I was lucky enough to get the idea quite easily, and was able to solve the question. After finishing all the parts on Q3, I went back to the MCQ questions I had left for later, and tried them again.

So that was my strategy: try the hard ones first, if you get stuck, move on, come back to them later. The MAT gives you 2.5 hours to attempt 10 MCQ and 4 long-answer questions. We suggest splitting your time as follows:

1.2. PREPARATION

1. **5** minutes per short question, totalling 50 minutes on Question 1.

2. **25** minutes per long question.

But you might find some questions easier than others, and some significantly harder, so you should be flexible with how you distribute your time on different problems.

During the exam

This 2-hours and 30-minutes exam is what you've prepared for, and for so long, but don't let the pressure get to you. Relax and enjoy the questions. After all, enjoying math is what led you here.

Here are our suggestions for approaching the exam.

Before you start working

Before you start thinking about the questions, glance over the questions to see if there's something interesting like that one automaton problem you did previously, or if there is something really nasty like a complicated integration problem. Then make an ordering of the questions according to which one you should attempt first. Knowing what lies ahead will give you a sense of confidence that helps a lot during exams like this.

So once you get the questions,

1. Glance over all the questions quickly
   a) scan for questions that look familiar
   b) try to identify questions that you might struggle with
2. Sort the questions in the increasing order of difficulty
3. Form a time-management strategy for the questions, based on their difficulty.
4. Start with the short questions.

What to do if you get stuck

Should you get stuck, which I believe almost everyone does at some point during the exam, it is better to move on to the next question instead of spending more time on the troubling parts. In my experience, when you get stuck on a question, it is because your mind can't come up with new ideas, and so you get into a loop of the same few ideas none of which work. So not only do you save time by moving on to a new question, you also get a way to escape the loop. When you go back to this question, you'll see that you can come up with new ideas almost always.

It is common to find yourself attempting approaches that do not yield any logical answers. In these cases, we suggest maximising your score by doing the following.

1. If you get stuck on problem, don't spend more time on it. Move on.

2. Try to save time in other questions so that you can go back to it at the end of the exam.

Often, candidates get stuck on a question due to unilateral thought. By moving on and attempting other questions, you give yourself a chance to re-approach the problematic question with renewed ideas.

Check your paper before the time runs out.

So 2 hours 20 minutes have passed! Now it's time to take a little one minute gap and go back to see what you've written so far and if you have missed any question you have skipped accidentally. Redoing a whole question at this point is impractical, but if you notice any easily fixable error in your solutions, this is the time to fix them.

Also, even if you don't know the correct solution to any of the MCQ questions, do not leave them blank, as there is no penalty for incorrect answers.

1. If you are done with most of the paper except for the ones that you skipped over, now is the time to go back to those problems.

2. If you are done with all the questions and there are still a couple of minutes left, go over your solution script to check for potential mistakes. You should pay attention to:

   a) Whether you have answered all of the questions

   b) Whether you wrote down the correct answer, specially in the short questions

3. If time is up, then it's time to relax! Take a deep breath and congratulate yourself!

CHAPTER 2

Strategies for problem solving

2.1 Where to begin

Questions on the MAT will not be your average exercises from A-levels (or equivalent) exams. You can be certain that almost all the time when you read the question statement, you won't know how to answer it immediately. How do you then go from reading the statement to solving the question?

Here enters the art of problem solving. The following section is an excerpt from Chapter 2, Section 2 of *"The Art and Craft of Problem Solving"* by *Paul Zeitz*, which we strongly recommend to the reader. It's an amazing book that introduces all the essential approaches and methods to solving mathematical (and other) problems.

Getting oriented

When you first read the question statement, you should

- Read the question carefully, paying attention to details such as positive vs. negative, etc.
- Begin to classify: is it a "to find" or "to prove" problem? Is the problem similar to others you have seen?
- Carefully identify the hypothesis and the conclusion.
- Try some quick preliminary brainstorming
  - Think about convenient notation.
  - Does a particular method of argument seem plausible?
  - Can you guess a possible solution? Trust your intuition.
  - Are there key words or concepts that seem important?

When you finish this (and don't rush), go back and do it again. It pays to reread a problem several times. As you rethink classification, hypothesis and conclusion, ask yourself if you can restate what you have already formulated. For example, it may seem that the hypothesis is really trivial, and you just repeat it verbatim from the statement of the problem. But if you try to restate it, you may discover new information.

When looking at the conclusion of the problem, especially a "to find" problem, sometimes it helps to "fantasise" an answer. Just make something up, and then reread the problem. Your fantasy answer is most likely false, and rereading the problem with this answer in mind may

2.1. WHERE TO BEGIN

help you to see why the answer is wrong, which may point out some of the more important constraints of the problem.

Don't spend too much time on orientation. You are done once you have a clear idea of what the problem asks and what the given is. Promising guesses about answers or methodology are bonuses, and nothing you should expect. Usually they require more intensive investigation.

I'm oriented, now what?

Get your hands dirty

This is easy and fun to do. Stay loose and experiment. Plug in lots of numbers. Keep playing around until you see a pattern. Then play around some more, and try to figure out why the pattern you see is happening. It is a well-kept secret that much high-level mathematical research is the result of low-tech "plug and chug" methods. The great Carl Gauss, widely regarded as one of the greatest mathematicians in history, was a big fan of this method. In one investigation, he painstakingly computed the number of integer solutions to $x^2 + y^2 < 90000$.

Penultimate step

Once you know what the desired conclusion is, ask yourself, "What will yield the conclusion in a single step?" Sometimes a penultimate step is "obvious," once you start looking for one. The more experienced you are, the more obvious the steps are.

For example, suppose that A and B are weird, ugly expressions that seem to have no connection, yet you must show that $A = B$. One penultimate step would be to argue separately that $A > B$ AND $B > A$. Perhaps you want to show instead that $A \neq B$. A penultimate step would be to show that A is always even, while B is always odd.

Always spend some time thinking very explicitly about possible penultimate steps. Of course, sometimes, the search for a penultimate step fails, and sometimes it helps one instead to plan a proof strategy.

Wishful thinking and Make it easier

These strategies combine psychology and mathematics to help break initial impasses in your work. Ask yourself, "What is it about the problem that makes it hard?" Then, make the difficulty disappear. You may not be able to do this legally, but who cares? Temporarily avoiding the hard part of a problem will allow you to make progress and may shed light on the difficulties.

For example, if the problem involves big, ugly numbers, make them small and pretty. If a problem involves complicated algebraic fractions or radicals, try looking at a similar problem without such terms. At best, pretending that the difficulty isn't there will lead to a bold solution. At worst, you will be forced to focus on the key difficulty of your problem, and possibly formulate an intermediate question, whose answer will help you with the problem at hand. Eliminating the hard part of a problem, even temporarily, will allow you to have some fun and raise your confidence. If you cannot solve the problem as written, at least you can make progress with its easier cousin.

2.2 Methods of Argument

Contradiction

Instead of trying to prove something directly, we start by assuming that it is false, and show that this assumption leads us to an absurd conclusion. A contradiction argument is usually helpful for proving that something cannot happen. Here is a simple example from number theory.

Example 2.1. $\sqrt{2}$ is irrational.

Proof. Seeking a contradiction, let us suppose that $\sqrt{2}$ is rational, that is, there are coprime integers p, q such that

$$\frac{p}{q} = \sqrt{2} \implies p^2 = 2q^2$$

Now that means 2 divides p^2, meaning p is even. So 4 divides p^2. That means 4 divides $2q^2$, implying q is also even. But we assumed that p, q are coprime.

So this is a contradiction, and $\sqrt{2}$ is not a rational number. □

When you start investigating a problem, always ask yourself if you could proceed by the way of contradiction. Check if you get important information when you negate the problem statement that might help with the investigation. In some questions, assuming the contrary to the statement provides more information than the original statement. Keep a vigilante eye out for these scenarios.

2.2. METHODS OF ARGUMENT

Standard Induction

Suppose we have a statement $P(n)$ that depends on the integer n. We want to prove the following assertion

$$\boxed{P(n) \text{ is true for all integers } n \geq n_0}$$

We prove the assertion with **standard** induction by showing the following:

Base case Establish the truth of $P(n_0)$. This is usually an easy exercise.

Inductive hypothesis Assume that $P(n)$ is true for some arbitrary integer n.

Inductive step Show that the inductive hypothesis implies that $P(n+1)$ is also true. This is usually the crucial part of the proof.

This is like the domino effect: the inductive step represents the fact that if one domino falls, the next will fall as well, and the base case represents knocking down the first domino.

Example 2.2. Prove that if n is an integer greater than 3, then $n! > 2^n$.

Proof. Base case: The base case is when $n = 4$. Which is obviously true:
$$4! = 24 > 16 = 2^4$$

Inductive hypothesis: For some integer $n \geq 4$, $n! > 2^n$.

Inductive step: We want to show $(n+1)! > 2^{n+1}$.

We already have (by our inductive hypothesis): $n! > 2^n$. Then,
$$(n+1)! = (n+1)n! > (n+1)2^n$$

Now, as $(n+1) > 4 > 2$, we have, $(n+1)2^n > 2^{n+1}$, hence
$$(n+1)! > 2^{n+1}$$

And by induction, we have that the result holds for all values of n. $\square$

Remark. The previous solution also shows how you usually structure your inductive argument

1. Prove the base case first.

2. State inductive hypothesis, and the inductive step.

3. Prove the inductive step.

You should also notice that the inductive step is where the main work of the proof is being done. Which is not surprising as this is the crucial step that makes the whole argument work.

Also, remember to always show the base case. Often it might seem like the base case is too trivial to bother writing it down – a perfect way to lose a point. Remember, no inductive argument is complete without the base case, and you should never neglect it.

Strong Induction

In weak induction, we assumed that the $P(n)$ holds for some n and showed that $P(n+1)$ also holds. But we can actually assume a stronger hypothesis, giving us the **Strong** induction.

Base case Establish the truth of $P(n_0)$ in the usual manner.

Inductive step Assume that $P(n_0), P(n_0+1), \ldots P(n-1), P(n)$ are all true for some arbitrary integer n. This is called the **strong inductive hypothesis**. Then show that the inductive hypothesis implies that $P(n+1)$ **is also true**.

Convince yourself that the two hypotheses of the weak and strong induction are equivalent. Therefore, it's never a bad idea to assume the strong induction hypothesis when arguing by induction. Having more information on your side can never go wrong.

> **Example 2.3.** Let the sequence $a_0, a_1, a_2, \ldots$ satisfy $a_0 = 0, a_1 = 1$ and
> $$a_{m+n} + a_{m-n} = \frac{1}{2}(a_{2m} + a_{2n})$$
> Prove that $a_n = n^2$.

Proof. Base case: $a_0 = 0^2 = 0$.

Strong inductive hypothesis: For all $k = 0, 1, 2, \ldots u$, $a_k = k^2$.

Inductive step: Show that $a_{u+1} = (u+1)^2$

Let $m = u, n = 1$. Then we have

$$a_{u+1} + a_{u-1} = \frac{1}{2}(a_{2u} + a_2) = \frac{1}{2}(4a_u + a_2) = 2a_u + 2$$

2.2. METHODS OF ARGUMENT

Now our stronger inductive hypothesis allows us to use the truth of both $P(u)$ and $P(u-1)$, so

$$a_{u+1} + (u-1)^2 = 2u^2 + 2$$

And hence,

$$a_{u+1} = 2u^2 + 2 - (u^2 - 2u + 1) = u^2 + 2u + 1 = (u+1)^2$$

By strong induction, it follows that $a_n = n^2$ for all $n \geq 0$. □

Extreme Principle

If possible, assume that the elements of your problem are "in order". Focus on the "largest" and "smallest" elements, as they may be constrained in interesting ways.

This might sound dull and not useful, but this simple idea is the key to solving problems in many situations, especially when proving a contradiction, or showing the existence of something.

> **Example 2.4.** Let B and W be finite sets of black and white points, respectively, in the plane, with the property that every line segment that joins two points of the same colour contains a point of the other colour. Prove that both sets must lie on a single line segment.

Proof. After experimenting, it seems that if the points do not all lie on a single line, there cannot be finitely many of them.

Assume that the points do not all lie on a line (Argument by contradiction.)

Then they form at least one triangle. Consider the triangle of **smallest area**.

At least two of its vertices have the **same colour**, so between them is a point of the other colour, but this forms a smaller triangle – a contradiction! Hence all the points must lie on a single line. □

Extreme principle is specially useful in proving a contradiction, or constructing an example. The rule of thumb is, if there is too much information in the statement, focus on what is important: the extreme elements.

Invariants and Monovariants

Invariants

An invariant, as the name suggests, is merely some aspect of a problem, usually a numerical quantity, that does not change, even if many other properties do change.

Here are a few examples of invariants:

1. The distance between two points on a number line is not changed by adding the same quantity to both numbers.

2. Let $s(n)$ be the sum of the digits of the base-ten representation of the positive integer n. Then $n - s(n)$ is always divisible by 9.

3. The ratio of the circumference to the diameter of a circle is invariant, that is π.

Invariants are very important in situations where at each step some complicated actions are being made, and we want to show some assertion about the result.

> **Example 2.5.** At first, a room is empty. Each minute, either one person enters or two people leave. After exactly 3^{1999} minutes, could the room contain $3^{1000} + 2$ people?

Solution. If there are n people in the room, after one minute, there will be either $n+1$ or $n-2$ people. The difference between these two possible outcomes is 3. Continuing for longer times, we see that

At any fixed time t, all the possible values for the population of the room differ from one another by multiples of 3.

In 3^{1999} minutes, then, one possible population of the room is just 3^{1999} people. This is a multiple of 3, so **all** the possible populations for the room have to also be multiples of 3. Therefore $3^{1000} + 2$ will not be a valid population. □

Monovariants

A monovariant is a quantity that may or may not change at each step of a problem, but when it does change, it does so monotonically: either it **increases or decreases**.

Monovariants are specially useful in showing that a process terminates:

2.2. METHODS OF ARGUMENT

If we can find a positive integer monovariant of a process that strictly decreases with every move, then we know it will eventually stop, because a positive integer can't decrease infinitely!

Example 2.6. In an elimination-style tournament of a two-person game, once you lose, you are out, and the tournament proceeds until only one person is left. Find a formula for the number of games that must be played in an elimination-style tournament starting with n contestants.

Solution. The number of people who are left in the tournament is clearly a monovariant over time. This number decreases by **one** each time a game is concluded.

So if we start with n people, the tournament must end after exactly $n-1$ games. □

MAT Specific Tips

On the MAT, you'll encounter questions that take the A-level syllabus, and adds the problem solving aspect to it. MAT questions have a very distinctive pattern that you can easily recognise, and strategise for. Here are some tips for just that:

1. In the MCQ section, process of elimination can be a powerful tool. Try to cancel out options that are obviously wrong. In some questions, you might be able to plug in the options into the statement to test if they are correct or not. This might potentially save you the trouble of lots of computation.

2. In MAT long questions, the questions are broken into parts, and the parts always somehow build up on the parts preceding them

    a) Either by directly using a result from a previous part, or

    b) by using the previous part as a hint.

3. In either case, always try to apply the techniques used in solving the previous parts of the questions.

4. If you can't give a full solution to a part of the question, that doesn't affect the other parts. So even if you haven't proved some part, you can use it's result in later parts.

5. Each part of a question is graded separately, but the score assigned to each part is not always indicative of the difficulty of the part.

2.3 Walkthrough: MAT 2010 Question 6

Now let us use the methods we learned to tackle an actual question from the MAT. Before reading the solution, we expect you to spend at least half an hour on this question.

Question

> In the questions below, the people involved make statements about each other. Each person is either a saint (S) who always tells the truth or a liar (L) who always lies.
>
> Six people, $P_1, P_2, \ldots, P_6$ sit in order around a circular table with P_1 sitting to P_6's right, as shown in the diagram below.
>
> **i.a** Suppose all six people say "the person directly opposite me is telling the truth". One possibility is that all six are lying. But, in total, how many different possibilities are there? Explain your reasoning.
>
> **i.b** Suppose now that all six people say "the person to my left is lying". In how many different ways can this happen? Explain your reasoning.
>
> Now n people $Q_1, Q_2, \ldots, Q_n$ sit in order around a circular table with Q_1 sitting to Q_n's right.
>
> **ii.a** Suppose that all n people make the statement "the person on my left is lying and the person on my right is telling the truth". Explain why everyone is lying.
>
> **ii.b** Suppose now that every person makes the statement "either the people to my left and right are both lying or both are telling the truth". If at least one person is lying, show that n is a multiple of three.

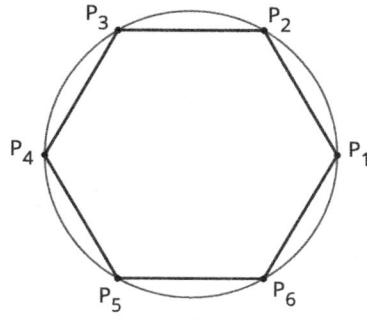

Figure 2.1

Solution

> (i.a) Suppose all six people say "the person directly opposite me is telling the truth". One possibility is that all six are lying. But, in total, how many different possibilities are there? Explain your reasoning.

Solution. The 6 people splits into 3 pairs sitting opposite to one another. For consistency each pair has to be both lying or both telling the truth.

Since one pair telling the truth or lying doesn't affect the other pairs, every possible combination of lies of truths are possible.

Hence there are a total of $2^3 = 8$ possible ways in which the statements can be made, considering two options for each of the three pairs. □

> (i.b) Suppose now that all six people say "the person to my left is lying". In how many different ways can this happen? Explain your reasoning.

Solution. If P_1 is telling the truth then P_6 is lying. If P_6 is lying, then by their statement, P_5 is telling the truth.

The only way that the statements can be made is as *SLSLSL* or *LSLSLS*. That is there are two ways. □

> Now n people $Q_1, Q_2, \ldots, Q_n$ sit in order around a circular table with Q_1 sitting to Q_n's right.
>
> (ii.a) Suppose that all n people make the statement "the person on my left is lying and the person on my right is telling the truth". Explain why everyone is lying.

Solution. If a particular person is a saint, then the person to their left is a liar and the person to the right is a saint, and we have a *LSS* situation, counting left-to-right to the saint and neighbours. If not then the person is a liar, and the possibilities for their neighbours are *LLL, SLS, SLL*.

Let's examine each possibility separately:

1. *LSS* situation: The left neighbour of the rightmost saint is a saint, which contradicts with their statement.

2. *SLS* situation: similarly is impossible, as the right neighbor of a saint must also be a saint.

3. *SLL* situation: is impossible as it only propagates by *LLL* and there is no means to complete the circle.

Hence, the only possibility is *LL...L* (*n* times). □

> (ii.b) Suppose now that every person makes the statement "either the people to my left and right are both lying or both are telling the truth". If at least one person is lying, show that n is a multiple of three.

Solution. If a person is a saint we are in a *SSS* or *LSL* situation; if not we are in an *LLS* or *SLL* situation.

1. *SSS* situation: can only consistently propagate as *SSS...S* and no-one would be lying.

2. *LLS* situation: can propagate to a *LSL*, then to a *SLL*, then to *LLS* etc. So the situation around the table can be *LLSLLSLLS...LLS*, that is any number of repeats of *LLS* (or equivalently of *LSL* or *SLL*), provided of course that n is a multiple of 3.

□

CHAPTER 3

Algebra

3.1 Logarithm

Logarithm is a very important topic on the MAT syllabus. We write $\boxed{\log_a x = y \text{ if } a^y = x}$ and read it as "log of x with base a is y". The following laws apply to log:

Exponentiation $a^{\log_a x} = x$

Multiplication $\log_a(xy) = \log_a x + \log_a y$

Division $\log_a\left(\frac{x}{y}\right) = \log_a x - \log_a y$

A special case occurs when $x = 1$ and $\log_a \frac{1}{x} = -\log_a x$

Exponent $\log_a(x^c) = c \log_a x$

Inverse $\log_a b = \dfrac{1}{\log_b a}$

Change of base $\log_a c = \log_a b \cdot \log_b c$

A special case of logarithms is when the base is e, and then we use the symbol $\ln x = \log_e x$. This is known as the natural log.

Some properties of logarithm

1. $\log_a$ is a scaled function of $\ln$: $\log_a x = \log_a e \times \ln x = \frac{1}{\ln a} \ln x$

2. Logarithm can be used to turn a long multiplication into addition
$$a_1 \cdot a_2 \cdot \ldots a_n = m \Leftrightarrow \ln a_1 + \ln a_2 + \cdots + \ln a_n = \ln m$$

3. Logarithm is only defined for positive numbers, so be careful of the sign of x before writing $\ln x$.

4. Logarithm is an **increasing** function. So $x < y \Leftrightarrow \ln x < \ln y$.

5. $\log x$ takes values between $(-\infty, \infty)$, and the only root of this function is 1.

6. When you see numbers like 2 and 8 together, you should be able to spot $8 = 2^3$. Similarly, noticing $4 = 2^2$, $16 = 4^2 = 2^4$, $9 = 3^2$, $27 = 3^3$ etc. will help you simplify some equations.

3.1. LOGARITHM

Example 3.1 (Inspired from MAT 2015 Question 1.H). How many distinct solutions does the following equation have?
$$\log_{x^2-1}\left(1-6x^2-5x^3\right)=2$$

Solution. We rewrite the equation in terms of exponents and get
$$1-6x^2-5x^3=(x^2-1)^2=x^4-2x^2+1 \implies x^4+5x^3+4x^2=0$$

Now, factoring this polynomial gives us
$$x^2(x^2+5x+4)=0 \implies x^2(x+4)(x+1)=0$$

Which we solve to get the solutions 0, -1 and -4. □

Example 3.2 (Inspired from MAT 2011 Question 1.H). What is the number of *positive* values of x that satisfy the equation
$$x^2 = 8^{\log_2 x} + 9^{\log_3 x + \frac{1}{2}} - 2^{\log_2 x} - \log_{\frac{1}{2}} \frac{1}{4}?$$

Solution. We can rewrite $8 = 2^3, 9 = 3^2, \frac{1}{4} = \frac{1}{2}^2$, so we have
$$8^{\log_2 x} = 2^{3\log_2 x} = 2^{\log_2 x^3} = x^3, \quad 9^{\log_3 x + \frac{1}{2}} = 3^{2\log_3 x + 1} = 3 \cdot 3^{\log_3 x^2} = 3x^2$$
$$2^{\log_2 x} = 2^{\log_2 x} = x$$

Putting these together in the equation gives us
$$x^2 = x^3 + 3x^2 - x + 2$$
$$\implies x^3 + 2x^2 - x + 2 = x^2(x+2) - 1(x+2) = (x+1)(x-1)(x+2) = 0$$

which has 1 *positive* solutions. (Careful! There was a trap here.) □

Tips for solving equations involving exponents

1. When there are terms like ab^x, it is often useful to take logarithm of the terms, so you get something like $\ln a + x \ln b$.

2. But be careful about additions of two terms! $\ln(a+b) \neq \ln a + \ln b$

3. It is often useful to think about the sizes of the terms involved. For example, if you have an equation like $2^x = x^2 + x$, then you know for sure the solutions, if there are any, will have to be quite small. This is because exponential functions grow much faster than polynomial functions.

> **Example 3.3** (Inspired from MAT 2019 Question 1.I). How many pairs of positive real numbers x and y satisfy $0 < x < y$ and
> $$x \ln x = y \ln y?$$

Solution. First notice the condition about x, y. We are given $0 < x < y$. So we can write $y = x + c$ for some positive number c. So this gives:

$$x \ln x = (x+c) \ln(x+c)$$

Now, notice that since ln is an increasing function, $\ln x < \ln(x+c)$ as c is positive. Also, $x < x + c$. So the right side is always strictly larger than the left side, hence there is no solution to the equation. $\square$

3.2 Solving Inequalities

If x, y are two real numbers and $x < y$, then

Addition $x + c < y + c$ for all real number c

Multiplication $xc < yc$ for all $c > 0$, and $xc > yc$ for all $c < 0$. (Be careful of multiplication of inequalities by negative numbers)

Inverse If $x \neq 0, y \neq 0, \frac{1}{x} > \frac{1}{y}$

The last two laws are the most important, as students often multiply inequalities by some negative number but forget to change the sign, which makes the resulting inequality wrong.

A few more useful rules to know: If $x < y$, then

Integers $x^n < y^n$ for all positive odd integers n. For the same to hold for positive even integers, we must have $|x| < |y|$.

Logarithm If $0 < x < y$, then $\ln x < \ln y$

3.2. SOLVING INEQUALITIES

Exponentiation If $x < y$, then $e^x < e^y$. Similarly for an $a > 1$, $a^x < a^y$, and for $0 \leq a < 1$, $a^x > a^y$.

Factorisation If $ab < 0$, then either $a < 0, b > 0$ or $a > 0, b < 0$.
If $ab > 0$, then either $a > 0, b > 0$ or $a < 0, b < 0$.

Absolute value If $|a| < c$, then $-c < a < c$. So we need to solve both of these inequalities separately.

Tips

When solving questions involving inequalities, it's often useful to

1. Bring all the terms to one side of the inequality.

2. If the inequality involves fractions, try to rearrange it so that it doesn't have fractions.

3. Consider the inequalities as equations. This is because we can add any number to inequalities and divide them by positive numbers without changing the sign.

4. In inequalities involving polynomials, usually the solution space will be an interval. Thinking about the roots of the interval and the sign of the terms help in solving these problems.

5. In inequalities involving trigonometric functions, it is useful to plot the involved functions. Bear in mind that solutions to inequalities of trigonometric functions usually are intervals.

> **Example 3.4.** Solve the inequality $\frac{1}{x} > x$, where $x \neq 0$.

Solution. This example shows the danger of solving inequalities exactly in the same way as we solve equations. If we were to multiply both sides by x and solve $1 > x^2$, we would get the solution $-1 \leq x \leq 1$. But, if x is negative, multiplying both sides would have flipped the sign of the inequality, and hence the range $-1 \leq x < 0$ is actually not a solution!

So we need to check both cases separately:

1. $x > 0$: This case we can solve by multiplying by x, and we get $0 < x < 1$ since $x^2 < 1$

2. $x < 0$: We need to flip the sign of the inequality. Multiplying both sides by x, we get: $x^2 > 1$. Which holds for $x < -1$

Hence our solution: $x < -1$ or $0 < x < 1$

Alternatively, we could multiply both sides by x^2, which is always positive, to get $x > x^3 \implies x^3 - x < 0 \implies x(x^2 - 1) < 0$. We have two cases

1. $x < 0$ and $x^2 - 1 > 0$: Gives $x < -1$

2. $x > 0$ and $x^2 - 1 < 0$: Gives $0 < x < 1$

Alternatively, we could solve this by looking at the graph of x^3 and x as well, which is always a quick intuitive way of solving inequalities

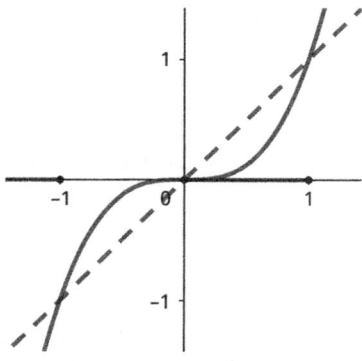

Figure 3.1: Solution is when the line of x is above the curve of x^3

□

Example 3.5. When is the inequality $x^4 < 5x^2 - 4$ satisfied?

Solution. First, we rearrange the inequality to bring everything to one side and factorise the polynomial
$$x^4 - 5x^2 + 4 < 0 \implies (x^2 - 4)(x^2 - 1) < 0$$

So we have either $x^2 - 4 < 0, x^2 - 1 > 0$ or $x^2 - 4 > 0, x^2 - 1 < 0$. Only one of these cases can be true, that is, $1 < x^2 < 4$, and that gives us
$$1 < x^2 < 4 \implies -2 < x < -1 \text{ or } 1 < x < 2$$

□

Example 3.6. Solve $|x^2 - 5x| < 4$.

Solution. Expanding the absolute value, we get $-4 < x^2 - 5x < 4$. Rearranging the first inequality gives $x^2 - 5x + 4 > 0$. Which rearranges to $(x-4)(x-1) > 0$. So, either $(x-4 < 0, x-1 < 0 \implies x < 4, x < 1$ or $x-4 > 0, x-1 > 0 \implies x > 1, x > 4$. So the two solutions are $x < 1$ or $x > 4$.

The second inequality gives $x^2 - 5x - 4 < 0$. Which rearranges to $(x-p)(x-q) < 0$ where

$$p = \frac{5 - \sqrt{41}}{2} \text{ and } q = \frac{5 + \sqrt{41}}{2}$$

Which gives the solution $p < x < q$.

Now, since the two inequalities need to hold simultaneously, we get the solution: $p < x < 1$ or $4 < x < q$.

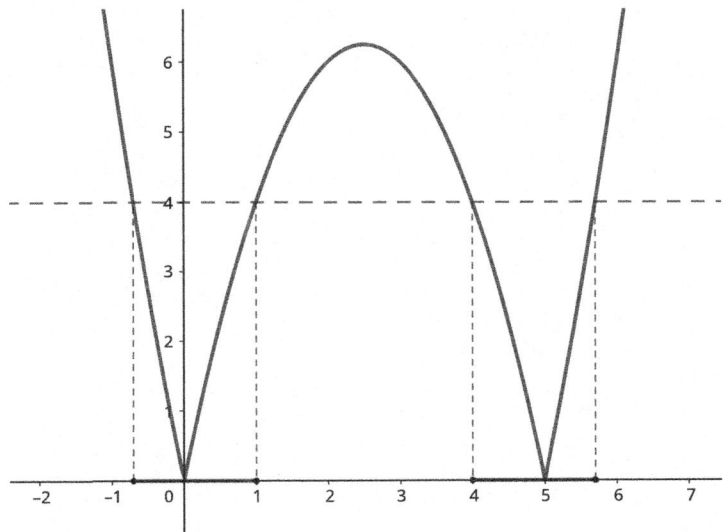

Figure 3.2

$\square$

3.3 Bounding

A typical bounding question will ask you to bound a variable x by some value y, that is, given a property that x satisfies, find y such that or, prove that $x \leq y$ for all such x. In these kinds of problems it's helpful to:

1. Replace terms by their given bounds and make the expression simpler. For example, if you're bounding $x^3 + hx^2 + h$, where $h < 1$, we can say $x^3 + hx^2 + h < x^3 + x^2 + 1$

2. Discard insignificant terms. For example, if $n > 1$, we can write $n^3 + 1 > n^3$, which makes the lower bound simpler to work with.

3. The quadratic polynomial gives some useful bounds on the coefficients: If $ax^2 + bx + c > 0$ for all x, then we know, the polynomial has no solution, hence the determinant $b^2 - 4ac < 0$. Also, $a > 0$ as otherwise the graph of the polynomial would be upside down.

> **Example 3.7** (MAT 2009 Question 3.iv rephrased). Let A, B be positive constants that satisfy
> $$\frac{1}{4n-1} - \frac{1}{n} \leq 2 - \frac{A}{n+B}$$
> for all $n \geq 1$. Show that $A \leq \frac{3}{4}$.

Solution. We first get rid of the fractions, and bring everything not involving A to one side:

$$\frac{1}{4n-1} - \frac{1}{n} \leq 2 - \frac{A}{n+B} \implies \frac{3n-1}{n(4n-1)} \geq \frac{A}{n+B}$$
$$\implies (3n-1)(n+B) \geq A(4n-1)n$$
$$\implies 3n^2 - n - B + 3Bn \geq 4An^2 - An$$

We then rearrange a bit further, and get

$$(3-4A)n^2 + (3B+A-1)n - B \geq 0 \text{ for } n \geq 1$$

This is the equation of a parabola in variable n, which is greater or equal than 0 for all $n \geq 1$. So the coefficient of n^2 must be positive, otherwise we know that the parabola would be "upside-down".

So the coefficient of n^2 must be positive, hence,

$$3 - 4A \geq 0 \implies A \leq \frac{3}{4}$$

$\square$

3.4 Walkthrough: MAT 2021 Question 2

Question

3.4. WALKTHROUGH: MAT 2021 QUESTION 2

It is given to you that

$$\ln(1-x) = -x - \frac{x^2}{2} - \frac{x^3}{3} - \frac{x^4}{4} \cdots - \frac{x^n}{n} \cdots \quad \text{for any } x \text{ with } |x| < 1$$

[Note that $\ln x$ is the natural log with base e: $\log_e x$.]

Part i. By choosing a particular value of x with $|x| < 1$, show that

$$\ln 2 = \frac{1}{2} + \frac{1}{2 \times 2^2} + \frac{1}{3 \times 2^3} + \frac{1}{4 \times 2^4} + \frac{1}{5 \times 2^5} + \cdots$$

Part ii. Use part (i) and the fact that

$$\frac{1}{n2^n} < \frac{1}{3 \times 2^n} \quad \text{for } n \geq 4$$

to find the integer k such that $\frac{k}{24} < \ln 2 < \frac{k+1}{24}$.

Part iii. Show that

$$\ln\left(\frac{3}{2}\right) = \frac{1}{2} - \frac{1}{2 \times 2^2} + \frac{1}{3 \times 2^3} - \frac{1}{4 \times 2^4} + \frac{1}{5 \times 2^5} - \cdots$$

and deduce that

$$\ln 3 = 1 + \frac{1}{3 \times 2^2} + \frac{1}{5 \times 2^4} + \frac{1}{7 \times 2^6} + \cdots$$

Part iv. Deduce that $\frac{13}{12} < \ln 3 < \frac{11}{10}$.

Part v. Which is larger: 3^{17} or 4^{13} ? Without calculating either number, justify your answer.

Solution

(Part i) By choosing a particular value of x with $|x| < 1$, show that

$$\ln 2 = \frac{1}{2} + \frac{1}{2 \times 2^2} + \frac{1}{3 \times 2^3} + \frac{1}{4 \times 2^4} + \frac{1}{5 \times 2^5} + \cdots$$

Solution. The first paragraph strongly suggests that we use the given formula. So what is the value of x that we need to consider?

In the given equation with $\ln(1-x)$, the right-hand side are all negatives. So we multiple the equation with $\ln 2$ by -1, and get

$$-\ln 2 = \ln\left(\frac{1}{2}\right) = -\frac{1}{2} - \frac{1}{2 \times 2^2} - \frac{1}{3 \times 2^3} - \frac{1}{4 \times 2^4} - \cdots$$

Now, equating the left hand side of both equations, we realise, ideally, we want $\ln(1-x) = \ln\left(\frac{1}{2}\right)$, that is, we want $x = \frac{1}{2}$.

Setting this value of x in the given equation, we get

$$\ln\left(\frac{1}{2}\right) = -\frac{1}{2} - \frac{(1/2)^2}{2} - \frac{(1/2)^3}{3} - \frac{(1/2)^4}{4} - \cdots$$

which after rearranging gives us

$$\ln 2 = -\ln\left(\frac{1}{2}\right) = \frac{1}{2} + \frac{1}{2 \times 2^2} + \frac{1}{3 \times 2^3} + \frac{1}{4 \times 2^4} + \cdots$$

□

(Part ii) Use part (i) and the fact that

$$\frac{1}{n2^n} < \frac{1}{3 \times 2^n} \quad \text{for } n \geq 4$$

to find the integer k such that $\frac{k}{24} < \ln 2 < \frac{k+1}{24}$.

Solution. We want to use our result from (Part i) somehow. Using the given inequality $\frac{1}{n2^n} < \frac{1}{3 \times 2^n}$ for each $n \geq 4$, we get

$$\ln 2 = \frac{1}{2} + \frac{1}{2 \times 2^2} + \frac{1}{3 \times 2^3} + \frac{1}{4 \times 2^4} + \cdots$$
$$< \frac{1}{2} + \frac{1}{2 \times 2^2} + \frac{1}{3 \times 2^3} + \frac{1}{3 \times 2^4} + \frac{1}{3 \times 2^5} + \frac{1}{3 \times 2^6} + \cdots$$

This sum can be factored as

$$\frac{1}{2} + \frac{1}{8} + \frac{1}{3 \times 2^3}\left(1 + \frac{1}{2} + \frac{1}{2^2} + \cdots\right)$$

and the sum inside the brackets is the sum of the terms of a geometric progression and equals to 2, so this is

$$\frac{1}{2} + \frac{1}{8} + \frac{1}{3 \times 2^3}(2) = \frac{1}{2} + \frac{1}{8} + \frac{1}{12} = \frac{17}{24}$$

3.4. WALKTHROUGH: MAT 2021 QUESTION 2   35

So $\ln 2 < \frac{17}{24}$.

Now, note that, all the terms inside in the expansion of $\ln 2$ are positive. So, we can drop all the terms $\frac{1}{n2^n}$ with $n \geq 4$ and get the lower bound on $\ln 2$

$$\ln 2 > \frac{1}{2} + \frac{1}{2 \times 2^2} + \frac{1}{3 \times 2^3} = \frac{16}{24}$$

Which means, $\frac{16}{24} < \ln 2 < \frac{17}{24}$. So $k = 16$. $\square$

(Part iii) Show that

$$\ln\left(\frac{3}{2}\right) = \frac{1}{2} - \frac{1}{2 \times 2^2} + \frac{1}{3 \times 2^3} - \frac{1}{4 \times 2^4} + \frac{1}{5 \times 2^5} - \cdots$$

and deduce that

$$\ln 3 = 1 + \frac{1}{3 \times 2^2} + \frac{1}{5 \times 2^4} + \frac{1}{7 \times 2^6} + \cdots$$

Solution. To get an expression for $\ln(\frac{3}{2})$, we should have $(1-x) = \frac{3}{2}$. So, setting $x = -\frac{1}{2}$ in the given expression for $\ln(1-x)$ gives

$$\ln\left(\frac{3}{2}\right) = \frac{1}{2} - \frac{1}{2 \times 2^2} + \frac{1}{3 \times 2^3} - \frac{1}{4 \times 2^4} + \cdots$$

Now, the left hand side is $\ln\left(\frac{3}{2}\right) = \ln 3 - \ln 2$. So, we can add the expression for $\ln 2$ found in part (i) to the expression we've just found for $\ln(3/2)$ to get

$$\ln 3 = 1 + \frac{1}{3 \times 2^2} + \frac{1}{5 \times 2^4} + \frac{1}{7 \times 2^6} + \cdots$$

$\square$

(Part iv) Deduce that $\frac{13}{12} < \ln 3 < \frac{11}{10}$.

Solution. We have already seen a similar process of bounding the value of $\ln$. So we should find a bound for all the terms of the form $\frac{1}{n2^{n-1}}$ for larger values of n.

We notice that $\frac{1}{7 \times 2^6} < \frac{1}{5 \times 2^6}, \frac{1}{9 \times 2^8} < \frac{1}{5 \times 2^8}$ and so on for all $n > 5$.

So we write

$$\ln 3 < 1 + \frac{1}{3 \times 2^2} + \frac{1}{5 \times 2^4} + \frac{1}{5 \times 2^6} + \frac{1}{5 \times 2^8} + \cdots$$
$$= 1 + \frac{1}{3 \times 2^2} + \frac{1}{5 \times 2^4}\left(1 + \frac{1}{4} + \frac{1}{4^2} + \cdots\right)$$
$$= 1 + \frac{1}{12} + \frac{1}{80}\left(\frac{4}{3}\right) = \frac{11}{10}$$

so $\ln 3 < \frac{11}{10}$. Also note that the terms are all positive, so

$$\ln 3 > 1 + \frac{1}{3 \times 2^2} = \frac{13}{12}$$

$\square$

> (Part v) Which is larger: 3^{17} or 4^{13}? Without calculating either number, justify your answer.

Solution. Take logarithms base e. We're asked to compare $17 \ln 3$ against $13 \ln 4$ ($\ln x$ is an increasing function of x so it's sufficient to compare these).

We know that $17 \ln 3 > \frac{17 \times 13}{12}$ and that

$$13 \ln 4 = 26 \ln 2 < \frac{26 \times 17}{24} = \frac{13 \times 17}{12}$$

So putting it all together, $13 \ln 4 < \frac{17 \times 13}{12} < 17 \ln 3$. That means that $4^{13} < 3^{17}$. $\square$

3.5 Common traps

When dealing with questions involving equations and inequalities, you should look out for these common pitfalls:

1. Be careful about the conditions of the solutions asked in the question.

2. While copying the equation, be extra cautious with coefficients and their signs.

CHAPTER **4**

Geometry

4.1 Coordinate Geometry

Cartesian coordinate

In the Cartesian coordinate system, we denote every point on the plane by two coordinates (a,b). If two perpendicular lines are draw from the point onto the x and y axis,

1. a represents the signed length of the perpendicular to the y axis.
2. b represents the signed length of the perpendicular to the x axis.

We call the point $O(0,0)$ the origin of this system. Note that the points on the x axis have the form $(a,0)$, and the points on the y axis have the form $(0,b)$.

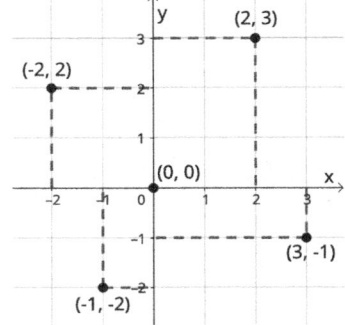

Figure 4.1

Polar coordinate

In Polar coordinates, we denote every point on the plane by two numbers (p, θ), where

1. p represents the distance of that point from the origin.

2. θ represents the angle created between the positive x axis and the line joining the point with the origin.

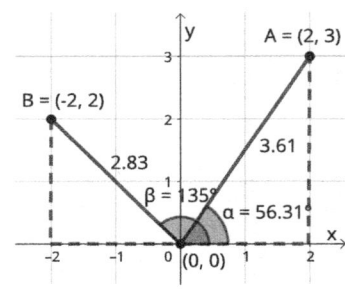

Figure 4.2

Changing between the two coordinates

Suppose a point (a,b) is given in Cartesian coordinate. We want to represent it in polar coordinates. If (p, θ) is the point in polar coordinates, by Pythagoras' theorem, we know

$$p = \sqrt{a^2 + b^2}$$
$$\cos \theta = \frac{a}{p}, \sin \theta = \frac{b}{p} \implies \tan \theta = \frac{b}{a} \implies \theta = \tan^{-1} \frac{b}{a}$$

And if (p, θ) is the point in polar coordinates, then the cartesian coordinate is given by (a,b) where

$$a = p \cos \theta, \ b = p \sin \theta$$

4.1. COORDINATE GEOMETRY

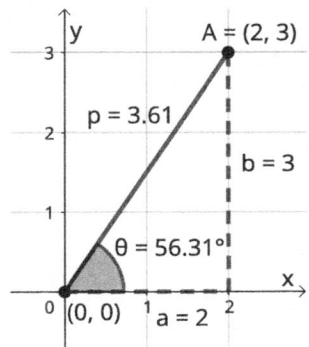

Figure 4.3

Distance and Gradient

Given two points with Cartesian coordinate $(x_1, y_1), (x_2, y_2)$, their distance

$$\sqrt{(x_1 - x_2)^2 + (y_1 - y_2)^2}$$

and the gradient of the line joining the two points

$$\tan \theta = m = \frac{y_1 - y_2}{x_1 - x_2}$$

Where θ is the angle produced by the line with the positive x direction.

Midpoint and Section Formula

Given two points with Cartesian coordinate $(x_1, y_1), (x_2, y_2)$, their midpoint has the coordinate

$$(x, y) = \left(\frac{x_1 + x_2}{2}, \frac{y_1 + y_2}{2} \right)$$

Now suppose we want to find the point that divides the line segment joining the two points in the ratio $m : n$. We have the following formula

$$(x, y) = \left(\frac{mx_2 + nx_1}{m + n}, \frac{my_2 + ny_1}{m + n} \right)$$

Example 4.1 (MAT Specimen b Question 1.A). What is the coordinate of the point lying between $P(2, 3)$ and $Q(8, -3)$ which divides the line PQ in the ratio $1 : 2$?

Solution. Using the section formula, we have $(x_1, y_1) = (2,3), (x_2, y_2) = (8,-3)$ and $m = 1, n = 2$. So the point has the coordinate

$$\left(\frac{1 \times 8 + 2 \times 2}{1+2}, \frac{1 \times -3 + 2 \times 2}{1+2}\right) = \left(4, \frac{1}{3}\right)$$

□

Example 4.2 (MAT 2020 Question 1.A). A square has centre $(3,4)$ and one corner at $(1,5)$. Another corner is at (a) $(1,3)$, (b) $(5,5)$, (c) $(4,2)$, (d) $(2,2)$, (e) $(5,2)$

Solution. We proceed by process of elimination. The distance from the centre to the corner is $\sqrt{5}$. That eliminates $(5,2)$.

Now if the corner opposite to $(1,5)$ is (a,b), then we have $a + 1 = 2 \times 3 \implies a = 5$, $b + 5 = 2 \times 4 \implies b = 3$. This is not one of the options, so the corner in the options is equidistant from these two points: $(1,5), (5,3)$.

Checking each point for this criteria, only $(2,2)$ satisfies it, hence it is our solution. □

Area of a triangle

Given a triangle ABC with the three vertices having coordinate $A = (x_1, y_1)$, $B = (x_2, y_2)$ and $C = (x_3, y_3)$, the area of the triangle is given by the formula

$$\Delta = \frac{1}{2} \begin{vmatrix} 1 & 1 & 1 \\ x_1 & x_2 & x_3 \\ y_1 & y_2 & y_3 \end{vmatrix}$$

Tips

1. Draw a graph with all the relevant points and segments.

2. When working with polar coordinates, it is often useful to first convert to Cartesian coordinates, switching back to Polar coordinates after the relevant calculations have been performed.

4.2 Lines and Vectors

4.2. LINES AND VECTORS

Equations of a line

The general equation of a line has the form

$$y = \underbrace{m}_{\text{gradient of the line}} x + \underbrace{c}_{\text{y-intercept}}$$

Because of its form $f(x) = mx + c$, a line is also called a linear function.

The gradient is sometimes called the slope of the line. If the line intersects x-axis at θ angle, then

$$\tan \theta = m = \frac{y_1 - y_2}{x_1 - x_2}$$

where $(x_1, y_1), (x_2, y_2)$ are two points on the line.

Other equations of lines

Depending on different situations when different sets of information are available, other representations of the linear equation might be useful. It's also helpful to know how to convert between any two of the following representations

1. Written as a single expression: $ax + by + c = 0$

2. Line passing through point (x_0, y_0) with slope m: $y = m(x - x_0) + y_0$

3. Line passing through two points $(x_1, y_1), (x_2, y_2)$: $\dfrac{y - y_1}{x - x_1} = \dfrac{y_1 - y_2}{x_1 - x_2}$

4. The line intersects x-axis at $(a, 0)$ and the y-axis at $(0, b)$: $\dfrac{x}{a} + \dfrac{y}{b} = 1$

5. The perpendicular from the origin to the line creates an angle θ, and the distance of the line from the origin is p: $x \cos \theta + y \sin \theta = p$

Perpendicular and Parallel lines

Let l_1, l_2 be two lines with respective equations $y = m_1 x + c_1$ and $y = m_2 x + c_2$. Then

1. l_1 is perpendicular to l_2 if $m_1 m_2 = -1$

2. l_1 is parallel to l_2 if $m_1 = m_2$

3. l_1, l_2 intersects at the point which is the solution to the equations $y - m_1 x = c_1$ and $y - m_2 x = c_2$

Perpendicular and parallel lines through a point

Given a line l with equation $y = mx + c$ and a point $P(x_0, y_0)$, we have

1. The line through P parallel to l: $y = y_0 + m(x - x_0)$
2. The line through P perpendicular to l: $y = y_0 - \dfrac{1}{m}(x - x_0)$

Tips

1. You can find the equation of a line if you have either of the two following pieces of information
   a) the gradient and one point that the line passes through.
   b) two points that the lines pass through.
2. Depending on the problem, finding one of these conditions will be easier than the other.
3. Remember the relation between differentiation and gradients: tangent line to the curve of a function $f(x)$ through the point $(x, f(x))$ has the slope $f'(x)$.

Vectors

On the Cartesian plane, a vector from $A = (x_1, y_1)$ to $B = (x_2, y_2)$ can be written as:

$$\vec{v} = \vec{AB} = (x_2 - x_1, y_2 - y_1) = (x_2 - x_1)\mathbf{i} + (y_2 - y_1)\mathbf{j}$$

where $\mathbf{i}, \mathbf{j}$ are the two directional unit vectors in x and y direction respectively.

We call the length of the vector its **magnitude**, which is

$$|\vec{v}| = \sqrt{(x_1 - x_2)^2 + (y_1 - y_2)^2}$$

We call the angle that the vector creates with the positive x-axis its **argument**. If the argument is θ, then we have

$$\tan \theta = \frac{y_2 - y_1}{x_2 - x_1}$$

We can write a vector in simpler terms with its x and y coordinates

$$\vec{v} = v_x \mathbf{i} + v_y \mathbf{j}$$

If we have two vectors $\vec{v} = v_x \mathbf{i} + v_y \mathbf{j}$, $\vec{w} = w_x \mathbf{i} + w_y \mathbf{j}$, we can,

4.2. LINES AND VECTORS

1. Add or subtract them
$$\vec{v} \pm \vec{w} = (v_x + w_x)\mathbf{i} \pm (v_y + w_y)\mathbf{j}$$

2. Multiply by a scalar $a \in \mathbb{R}$
$$a\vec{v} = (av_x)\mathbf{i} + (av_y)\mathbf{j}$$

and we have
$$|a\vec{v}| = a|\vec{v}|$$

Unit vectors

If a vector has length equal to 1, then we call it an unit vector. Given a vector $\vec{v}$, we can find the unit vector $\vec{u}$ that has the same direction as $\vec{v}$ by

$$\vec{u} = \frac{\vec{v}}{|\vec{v}|} = \frac{v_x}{\sqrt{v_x^2 + v_y^2}}\mathbf{i} + \frac{v_y}{\sqrt{v_x^2 + v_y^2}}\mathbf{j}$$

The unit vector that points to the direction θ angle from the x-axis can be written as

$$\vec{u} = \cos\theta \mathbf{i} + \sin\theta \mathbf{j}$$

Projection

Suppose we have two vectors $\vec{v}, \vec{w}$ from the same origin. They form an angle θ at the origin.

(a) Two vectors v, w   (b) Projection of v on w

Figure 4.4: Projection

The projection of $\vec{v}$ onto $\vec{w}$ can be found by drawing a perpendicular line from the endpoint of $\vec{v}$ to $\vec{w}$.

The length of the projection is given by

$$|\vec{u}| = |\vec{v}|\cos\theta$$

Dot product

The dot product between two vectors $\vec{v}, \vec{w}$ is given by

$$\vec{v} \cdot \vec{w} = |\vec{v}||\vec{w}|\cos\theta$$

where θ is the angle created by the two vectors when joined at the origin.

Hence the projection of v onto w can be thought of as the dot product of $\vec{v}$ and the unit vector to the direction of $\vec{w}$:

$$|\vec{v}|\cos\theta = \vec{v} \cdot \left(\frac{\vec{w}}{|\vec{w}|}\right)$$

If $\vec{v} = v_x\mathbf{i} + v_y\mathbf{j}$ and $\vec{w} = w_x\mathbf{i} + w_y\mathbf{j}$, then

$$|\vec{v}||\vec{w}|\cos\theta = \vec{v} \cdot \vec{w} = v_xw_x + v_yw_y$$

Which gives us a convenient way of finding the angle θ between the two vectors.

Tips

1. When working with vectors, it's always helpful to draw diagrams.

2. Remember the Sine and Cosine rules from trigonometry? You can use them to find lengths of vectors.

3. Sometimes switching between the coordinate form and the line form of the vector gives useful information.

Measuring distance

Distances from a point

The distance between two points $(x_1, y_1), (x_2, y_2)$ is

$$\sqrt{(x_1 - x_2)^2 + (y_1 - y_2)^2}$$

The distance between a line and a point, however, can be tricky to calculate. Let us see how to calculate it.

Distance to a line

4.3. WALKTHROUGH: MAT 2009 QUESTION 4

Theorem 4.1 (Distance from a point to a line) — Suppose a line l has the equation $ax + by + c = 0$. The perpendicular distance from a point $Q(x_0, y_0)$ to this line is

$$d = \frac{|a(x_0) + b(y_0) + c|}{\sqrt{a^2 + b^2}}$$

Proof. Pick one point $P(x_1, y_1)$ on l. Let $\vec{n}(a,b)$ be the vector perpendicular to the line at P. Let d be the perpendicular line from Q to l.

We see that d is the orthogonal projection of $\vec{PQ}$ over d. If θ is the angle between $\vec{PQ}$ and d, then

$$d = \left|\vec{PQ}\right| \cos\theta$$

Multiplying both sides by the magnitude of $\vec{n}$, we get

$$d = \frac{\left|\vec{PQ}\right| |\vec{n}| \cos\theta}{|\vec{n}|}$$

We know $\left|\vec{PQ}\right| |\vec{n}| \cos\theta = \vec{PQ} \cdot \vec{n}$. So

$$d = \frac{\vec{PQ} \cdot \vec{n}}{|\vec{n}|}, \text{ and } \vec{PQ} = (x_0 - x_1, y_0 - y_1)$$

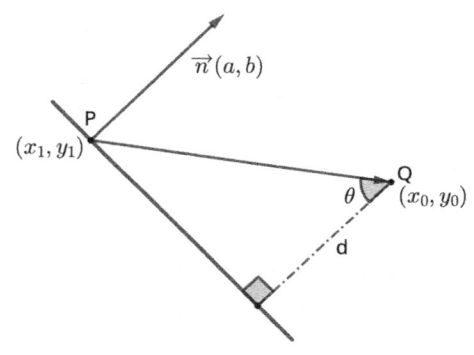

Figure 4.5

So,

$$\vec{PQ} \cdot \vec{n} = a(x_0 - x_1) + b(y_0 - y_1)$$

Now putting these together in an equation, we get

$$d = \frac{|a(x_0 - x_1) + b(y_0 - y_1)|}{\sqrt{a^2 + b^2}} = \frac{|ax_0 + by_0 + c|}{a^2 + b^2}$$

as $P \in l$, so $ax_1 + yx_1 + c = 0$. □

4.3 Walkthrough: MAT 2009 Question 4

Question

As shown in the diagram below: C is the parabola with equation $y = x^2$; P is the point $(0, 1)$; Q is the point (a, a^2) on C; L is the normal to C which passes through Q.

Part i. Find the equation of L.

Part ii. For what values of a does L pass through P?

Part iii. Determine $|QP|^2$ as a function of a, where $|QP|$ denotes the distance from P to Q.

Part iv. Find the values of a for which $|QP|$ is smallest.

Part v. Find a point R, in the xy-plane but not on C, such that $|RQ|$ is smallest for a unique value of a. Briefly justify your answer.

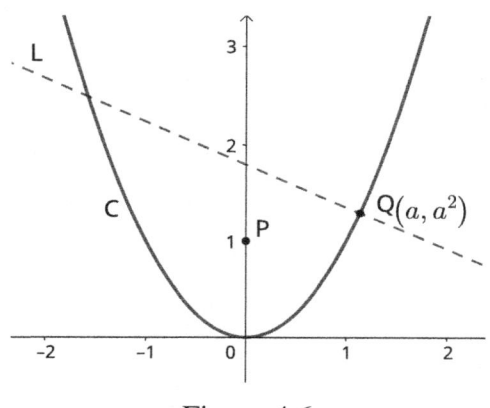

Figure 4.6

Solution

(Part i) Find the equation of L.

Solution. By definition, the normal line is perpendicular to the tangent line to C through Q. We can find the gradient of the normal line if we know the gradient of the tangent line by our previous discussion.

We can find the gradient of the tangent line by differentiating. At the point $Q(a, a^2)$, we know $f'(a) = 2a$. So, we know the gradient at Q is $2a$ and so the normal has gradient $-\frac{1}{2a}$. But this is only when $a \neq 0$.

4.3. WALKTHROUGH: MAT 2009 QUESTION 4

Hence the line L which passes through (a, a^2) and has gradient $-\frac{1}{2a}$ has the equation

$$y - a^2 = \frac{-1}{2a}(x - a) \implies x + 2ay = 2a^3 + a$$

And if $a = 0$, the tangent line is the x axis and the normal line is the y axis. □

(Part ii) For what values of a does L pass through P ?

Solution. So L passes through P if the point $(0, 1)$ satisfies the line equation

$$x + 2ay = 2a^3 + a$$

Which holds if,

$$0 + 2a = 2a^3 + a \implies a(2a^2 - 1) = 0 \implies a = \frac{\pm 1}{\sqrt{2}}, \text{ or } a = 0$$

□

(Part iii) Determine $|QP|^2$ as a function of a, where $|QP|$ denotes the distance from P to Q.

Solution. We know the coordinates of the two points, so finding the distance is straightforward.

$Q = (a, a^2)$ and $P = (0, 1)$. Hence, the distance $|PQ|^2$ is

$$|PQ|^2 = a^2 + (a^2 - 1)^2 = a^4 - a^2 + 1$$

□

(Part iv) Find the values of a for which $|QP|$ is smallest.

Solution. The minimum is achieved when the first derivative is zero. That is

$$4a^3 - 2a = 0 \implies a = 0, \frac{1}{\sqrt{2}}, \text{ or } \frac{-1}{\sqrt{2}}$$

But this method also gives us the other turning points. So we need to plug-in the three values into the function to see which one is the minimum. We see that 0 is a local maximum, and the minimum is achieved at the other two points.

So the minimum is when $a^2 = 1/2$ □

> (Part v) Find a point R, in the xy-plane but not on C, such that $|RQ|$ is smallest for a unique value of a. Briefly justify your answer.

Solution. We need to find a point R, in the xy-plane, such that there is a unique Q on C such that $|RQ|$ is the smallest.

So if we think of a circle expanding from R, the moment it first hits C, the circle should touch C. So where's a good place for R to be?

Anywhere underneath the graph of R! For a quick example, $R = (0, -1)$ satisfies our requirement. □

Remark. As an end note, if R is above the curve C, then there will always be two points on C such that $|RQ|$ is the smallest. Can you prove it?

4.4 Circles

Theorems on circles

Most of the following theorems are straightforward, and hence the details of the proofs are left to the reader as exercises. For most of the theorems however, an outline of the proof is given, and a "proof by figure" is also provided.

> **Theorem 4.2** (Chords and Tangents) — If A, B are two points on a circle centred at O, and if M is the midpoint of AB, then O is perpendicular to AB.
>
> The tangent to A is perpendicular to OA at A.

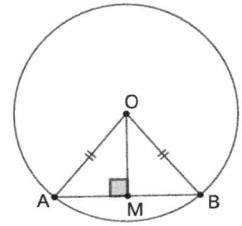

(a) Perpendicular to chord

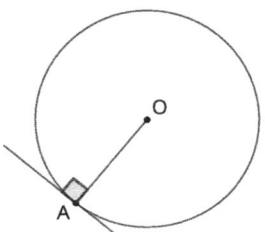

(b) Perpendicular to tangent

> **Theorem 4.3** (Angle at the centre) — If A, B, C are three points on a circle centred at O, and if C lies on the same side of the line AB as O, then $\angle AOB = 2\angle ACB$

Proof. Draw the line OC. Then consider the two isosceles triangles $\triangle AOC$ and $\triangle BOC$. □

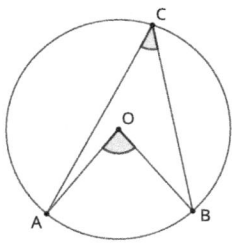

(a) Theorem

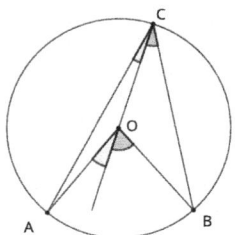

(b) Proof outline

> **Theorem 4.4** (Angle formed by a diameter) — If A, B, C are three points on a circle centred at O, and if AB is a diameter, $\angle ACB = 90°$

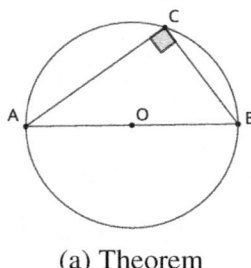

(a) Theorem

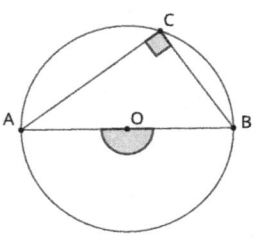

(b) Proof outline

Proof. Draw the line AB, it passes through O, so $\angle AOB = 180°$. Now apply the previous theorem. □

Theorem 4.5 (Angle on circle) — If A, B, C, D are four points on a circle centred at O, and if C lies on the same side of the line AB as D, then $\angle ACB = \angle ADB$

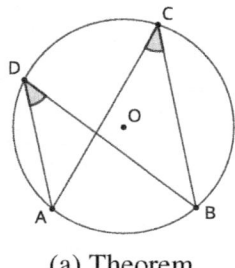

(a) Theorem

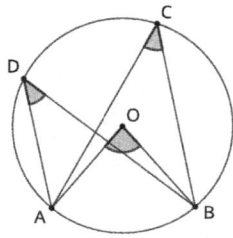

(b) Proof outline

Proof. Join O, A and O, B, then use the first theorem to get $\angle AOB = 2\angle ACB = 2\angle ADB$. □

Theorem 4.6 (Angles on quadrilateral) — If A, B, C, D is a quadrilateral on a circle centred at O, then $\angle ACB + \angle BDA = 180°$

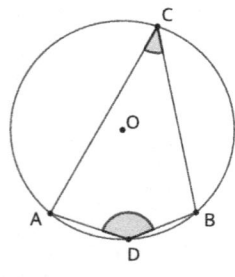

(a) Theorem

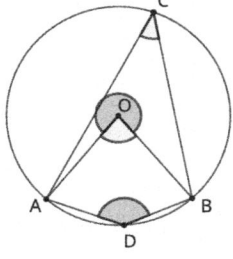

(b) Proof outline

4.4. CIRCLES

Proof. Join O,A and O,B, then use the first theorem to get $\angle AOB = 2\angle ACB$ and $\angle BOA = 2\angle ADB$ □

> **Theorem 4.7** (Tangents and alternate segment) — If A,B,C are three points on a circle centred at O, and C lies on the same side of the line AB as O. If EA is tangent to the circle, then $\angle EAB = \angle ACB$

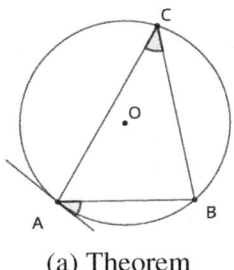

(a) Theorem

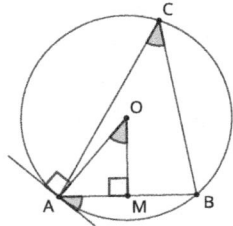

(b) Proof outline

Proof. Extend the tangent line to E. Draw the midpoint of AB, join it to O. Argue with angles $\angle EAB = 90 - \angle BAO = \angle AOM = \frac{1}{2}\angle AOB = \angle ACB$ □

Circle Equations

Circle equation

> **Theorem 4.8** (Circle Equation) — A circle with centre at (a,b) and radius r has the equation
> $$(x-a)^2 + (x-b)^2 = r^2$$

This form of the equation clearly indicates the centre and radius of the circle. In general, circle equations can be written simply as

> **Theorem 4.9** (General circle equation) — An equation $x^2 + y^2 + 2ax + 2by + c = 0$ represents a circle if $a^2 + b^2 - c > 0$. In that case, the centre of circle lies at $(-a,-b)$ and the radius is $\sqrt{a^2 + b^2 - c}$.

Tips

1. To find the equation of a circle, you must know it's centre and radius. If the equation is unknown, begin by finding these values first.

2. Remember the first two theorems:

    a) The line joining the centre and the midpoint of a chord is perpendicular to the chord

    b) The line joining the centre and a point on the circle is perpendicular to the line tangent to the circle through that point.

    They are often useful in determining the centre and/or the radius.

Example

> **Example 4.3** (MAT 2009 Question 1.B). What is the distance from the origin of the point on the following circle that is closest to the origin?
> $$x^2 + y^2 + 6x + 8y = 75$$

Solution. We rewrite the given equation in the simple form by completing the square:
$$x^2 + y^2 + 6x + 8y + 9 + 16 = 75 + 25 \implies (x+3)^2 + (y+4)^2 = 100$$

Hence the circle has centre $(-3, -4)$ and radius 10.

Note that, the point on the circle that is closest to the origin must lie on the line joining the origin and the centre of the circle.

Now, the radius from the centre, back through the origin, meets the circle at $(3, 4)$ which is at a distance 5 from the origin.

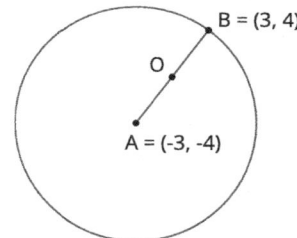

Figure 4.13

Hence the answer is 5. □

> **Example 4.4** (MAT 2011 Question 1.F). For which values of θ in the range $0 \leq \theta < \pi$ does the following equation represents a circle?
> $$x^2 + y^2 + 4x\cos\theta + 8y\sin\theta + 10 = 0$$

4.4. CIRCLES

Solution. Note that $x^2 + y^2 + 4x\cos\theta + 8y\sin\theta + 10 = 0$ rearranges to

$$(x + 2\cos\theta)^2 + (y + 4\sin\theta)^2 = 4\cos^2\theta + 16\sin^2\theta - 10 = 12\sin^2\theta - 6$$

so the equation defines a circle of radius $\sqrt{12\sin^2\theta - 6}$ provided $\sin^2\theta > \frac{1}{2}$.

In the given range, $0 \leqslant \theta < \pi$, we have $\sin\theta \geqslant 0$ and so we need $\frac{1}{\sqrt{2}} < \sin\theta$.

So we need $\theta > \frac{\pi}{4}$ and also $\theta < \frac{3\pi}{4}$ □

Tangents

Given a circle with equation $(x-a)^2 + (y-b)^2 = r^2$, and a point (x_0, y_0) on the circle, how do we find the equation of the line through (x_0, y_0) that is tangent to the circle?

We draw a line from the centre to the point, the tangent is perpendicular to this line. The slope of the line connecting the centre and the point is

$$m = \frac{y_0 - b}{x_0 - a}$$

Hence the slope of the tangent line is: $-\frac{1}{m} = \frac{x_0 - a}{y_0 - b}$

And the equation of the tangent is:

$$\frac{y - y_0}{x - x_0} = \frac{x_0 - a}{y_0 - b}$$

Measuring in circles

Radian measure

This topic has been removed from the MAT syllabus since 2018. But we recommend learning it as measuring and expressing angles in radian gives a natural way to study trigonometric functions.

Radian is a way to measure angles in terms of circular arc lengths. In this system

$$180° = \pi^c \text{ and } 1° = \frac{\pi}{180}^c$$

We use ^{c} notation to denote angles in radian measure.

A radian measure can be thought of as a length of an arc of a circle with a radius of 1 subtended by the angle. For example

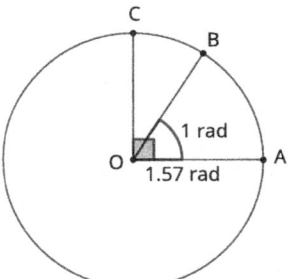

Figure 4.14: 1^c means the circular arc has length 1

Arc lengths

Because radian measure is measured in terms of circular arc lengths, inversely, we can measure the lengths of arcs in terms of angles in radian measure.

In this picture, r is the radius of the circle, a is the angle subtended by the arc of length s in radius measure. Then, $s = ra$.

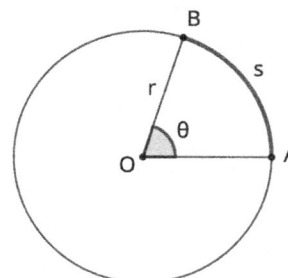

Figure 4.15

Area of sectors

Radian measure can also be used to measure the area of a sector.

In the picture, r is the radius of the circle, a is the angle of subtended by the arc of length s in radius measure. Then, the area of the sector is given by $\frac{1}{2}r^2 a$.

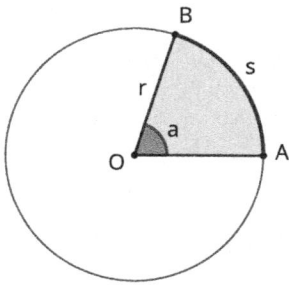

Figure 4.16

4.5 Walkthrough: MAT 2015 Question 4

Question

A circle A passes through the points $(-1,0)$ and $(1,0)$. Circle A has centre (m,h), and radius r.

Part i Determine m and write r in terms of h.

Part ii Given a third point (x_0, y_0) and $y_0 \neq 0$ show that there is a unique circle passing through the three points $(-1,0), (1,0), (x_0, y_0)$.

For the remainder of the question we consider three circles A, B, and C, each passing through the points $(-1,0), (1,0)$. Each circle is cut into regions by the other two circles. For a group of three such circles, we will say the "lopsidedness" of a circle is the fraction of the full area of that circle taken by its largest region.

Part iii Let circle A additionally pass through the point $(1,2)$, circle B pass through $(0,1)$, and let circle C pass through the point $(0,-4)$. What is the lopsidedness of circle A ?

Part iv Let $p > 0$. Now let A pass through $(1, 2p), B$ pass through $(0,1)$, and C pass through $(-1,-2p)$. Show that the value of p minimising the lopsidedness of circle B satisfies the equation

$$(p^2+1)\tan^{-1}\left(\frac{1}{p}\right) - p = \frac{\pi}{6}$$

Note that $\tan^{-1}(x)$ is sometimes written as $\arctan(x)$ and is the value of θ in the range $\frac{-\pi}{2} < \theta < \frac{\pi}{2}$ such that $\tan(\theta) = x$.

Solution

(Part i) Determine m and write r in terms of h.

Solution. By one of our circle theorems, we know that the centre must lie on the perpendicular bisector line of $(-1,0)$ and $(1,0)$, which is the y-axis. So $m = 0$.

Now from the circle equation, we know

$$r^2 = (x-m)^2 + (y-h)^2 = (1-m)^2 + h^2 = (-1-m)^2 + h^2$$

So, $r = \sqrt{1+h^2}$. □

(Part ii) Given a third point (x_0, y_0) and $y_0 \neq 0$ show that there is a unique circle passing through the three points $(-1, 0), (1, 0), (x_0, y_0)$.

Solution. Let (x_0, y_0) be our third point. Since we want this point on the circle, we must have,
$$(x_0 - m)^2 + (y_0 - h)^2 = r^2 = x_0^2 + (y_0 - h)^2$$
Expanding the right side gives us
$$r^2 = x_0^2 + y_0^2 - 2y_0 h + h^2$$
$$0 = -1 + x_0^2 + y_0^2 - 2y_0 h$$
Substituting in $h = \sqrt{r^2 - 1}$, gives
$$x_0^2 + y_0^2 = 1 + 2y_0 \sqrt{r^2 - 1}$$

Now, this is uniquely dependent on x_0 and y_0, so the circle with radius r is uniquely determined. □

(Part iii) Let circle A additionally pass through the point $(1, 2)$, circle B pass through $(0, 1)$, and let circle C pass through the point $(0, -4)$. What is the lopsidedness of circle A?

Solution. The lopsidedness of A is given by:

[area of circle $A = 2\pi$]

$-$[sector formed by points $(-1, 0)$ and $(1, 0)$ of circle $= \dfrac{\pi}{2}$]

$-$[triangle formed by centre of circle A and points $(-1, 0)$ and $(1, 0) = 1$]

$-$[semicircle of circle $B = \dfrac{\pi}{2}$]

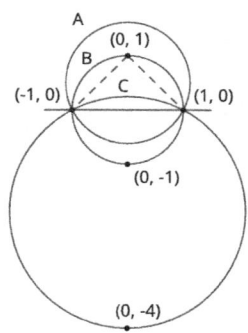

Figure 4.17

4.5. WALKTHROUGH: MAT 2015 QUESTION 4

Hence the lopsidedness $L(A)$ equals

$$L(A) = \frac{2\pi - \left(\frac{\pi}{2} - 1\right) - \frac{\pi}{2}}{2\pi} = \frac{\pi + 1}{2\pi}$$

□

Part iv (Part iv) Let $p > 0$. Now let A pass through $(1, 2p)$, B pass through $(0, 1)$, and C pass through $(-1, -2p)$. Show that the value of p minimising the lopsidedness of circle B satisfies the equation

$$(p^2 + 1) \tan^{-1}\left(\frac{1}{p}\right) - p = \frac{\pi}{6}$$

Note that $\tan^{-1}(x)$ is sometimes written as $\arctan(x)$ and is the value of θ in the range $\frac{-\pi}{2} < \theta < \frac{\pi}{2}$ such that $\tan(\theta) = x$.

Solution. Observe that the centre of A is at $(0, p)$ and the centre of C is at $(0, -p)$.

The lopsidedness of B is minimised when B is split into three equal regions (of area $\frac{\pi}{3}$).

The area of the middle region of B is the area of the two sectors formed by A and C minus the area of the two triangles formed by the centres of the circles A and C and the points $(-1, 0)$ and $(1, 0)$.

The line $y = 0$ splits this middle region precisely in two, so the difference between one sector and one triangle should be $\pi/6$.

Each sector has area $(p^2 + 1) \tan^{-1}\left(\frac{1}{p}\right)$ and each triangle has area p. Hence the lopsidedness is minimised when the equation is satisfied.

□

CHAPTER 5
Trigonometry

5.1 Definitions of Trigonometric Functions

Given a right-angled triangle $\triangle ABC$, and the lengths as shown on the figure, we define the trigonometric functions in terms of θ

$$\sin\theta = \frac{b}{a}, \quad \cos\theta = \frac{c}{a}, \quad \tan\theta = \frac{b}{c}$$

And,

$$\operatorname{cosec}\theta = \frac{a}{b}, \quad \sec\theta = \frac{a}{c}, \quad \cot\theta = \frac{c}{b}$$

By definition, we have the identities:

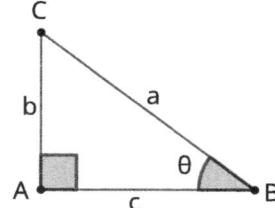

Figure 5.1

$$\operatorname{cosec}\theta = \frac{1}{\sin\theta}, \quad \sec\theta = \frac{1}{\cos\theta}, \quad \cot\theta = \frac{1}{\tan\theta}$$

Defining the trigonometric functions in terms of a right-angled triangle restricts the value $0 \leq \theta \leq 90$. But we can extend this definition to all values of θ

Let line OP create θ_1 angle with the positive x axis. Then,

$$\sin\theta_1 = \frac{PQ}{OP}, \quad \cos\theta = \frac{OQ}{OP}, \quad \tan\theta = \frac{PQ}{OQ}$$

Where the lengths are signed.

On the figure before, we see 4 angles in four different quadrants. Here,

- $0 \leq \theta_1 \leq \frac{\pi}{2}$: First quadrant. Here

$$\sin\theta_1 \geq 0, \cos\theta_1 \geq 0, \tan\theta_1 \geq 0$$

- $\frac{\pi}{2} \leq \theta_2 \leq \pi$: Second quadrant. Here

$$\sin\theta_2 \geq 0, \cos\theta_2 \leq 0, \tan\theta_2 \leq 0$$

- $\pi \leq \theta_3 \leq \frac{3\pi}{4}$: Third quadrant. Here

$$\tan\theta_3 \geq 0, \sin\theta_3 \leq 0, \cos\theta_3 \leq 0$$

- $\frac{3\pi}{4} \leq \theta_4 \leq 2\pi$: Fourth quadrant. Here

$$\cos\theta_4 \geq 0, \sin\theta_4 \leq 0, \tan\theta_4 \leq 0$$

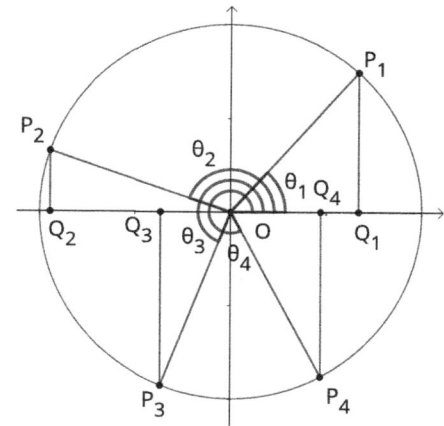

Figure 5.2

5.2 Basic Identities

Relations between $\sin, \cos, \tan$

For any θ, we have

1. $\sin\theta = \cos(90-\theta)$
2. $\tan\theta = \cot(90-\theta)$
3. $\sec\theta = \operatorname{cosec}(90-\theta)$

Also,

1. $\sin(-\theta) = -\sin\theta$
2. $\cos(-\theta) = \cos\theta$
3. $\tan(-\theta) = -\tan\theta$

And,

1. $\sin\theta = \sin(180-\theta)$
2. $\cos\theta = -\cos(180-\theta)$
3. $\tan\theta = -\tan(180-\theta)$

And,

1. $\sin(360+\theta) = \sin\theta$
2. $\cos(360+\theta) = \cos\theta$
3. $\tan(180+\theta) = \tan\theta$

Sum and Difference formulas

For any x, y, we have

1. $\sin(x \pm y) = \sin x \cos y \pm \cos x \sin y$
2. $\cos(x \pm y) = \cos x \cos y \mp \sin x \sin y$
3. $\tan(x \pm y) = \dfrac{\tan x \pm \tan y}{1 \mp \tan x \tan y}$

For any x,

1. $\sin 2x = 2 \sin x \cos x$
2. $\cos 2x = \cos^2 x - \sin^2 x = 2\cos^2 x - 1$
   $= 1 - 2\sin^2 x$
3. $\tan 2x = \dfrac{2 \tan x}{1 - \tan x}$

Product to sum formulas

We have

1. $2 \sin x \cos y = \sin(x+y) + \sin(x-y)$
2. $2 \sin x \sin y = \cos(x-y) - \cos(x+y)$
3. $2 \cos x \cos y = \cos(x+y) + \cos(x-y)$

Pythagorean identities and Periodicity

We also have the following very important identities for all x,

$$\sin^2 x + \cos^2 x = 1$$
$$\tan^2 x = 1 + \sec^2 x$$
$$\csc^2 x = 1 + \cot^2 x$$

$\sin, \cos$ are periodic function with period $360°$, or 2π, meaning,

$$\sin(x+360°) = \sin x, \quad \cos(x+360°) = \cos x$$

And, $\tan$ is also a periodic function with period $180°$.

Sine and Cosine rule

In a triangle $\triangle ABC$ with $BC = a, CA = b, AB = c$, and $\angle A = \angle BAC, \angle B = \angle ABC, \angle C = \angle ACB$, we have,

1. **Sine Rule:**
$$\frac{\sin \angle A}{a} = \frac{\sin \angle B}{b} = \frac{\sin \angle C}{c}$$

2. **Cosine Rules:**
$$c^2 = a^2 + b^2 - 2ab\cos \angle C$$
$$a^2 = b^2 + c^2 - 2bc\cos \angle A$$
$$b^2 = c^2 + a^2 - 2ca\cos \angle B$$

General solutions to $\sin, \cos, \tan$

The general solutions to the equation

1. $\sin x = \sin \theta$: $x = 180°n + (-1)^n \theta = n\pi + (-1)^n \theta$
2. $\cos x = \cos \theta$: $x = 360°n \pm \theta = 2n\pi \pm \theta$
3. $\tan x = \tan \theta$: $x = 180°n + \theta = n\pi + \theta$

for all integer n.

Useful values of sin, cos, tan

θ	0	$\dfrac{\pi}{6}$	$\dfrac{\pi}{4}$	$\dfrac{\pi}{3}$	$\dfrac{\pi}{2}$	π
$\sin\theta$	0	$\dfrac{1}{2}$	$\dfrac{1}{\sqrt{2}}$	$\dfrac{\sqrt{3}}{2}$	1	0
$\cos\theta$	1	$\dfrac{\sqrt{3}}{2}$	$\dfrac{1}{\sqrt{2}}$	$\dfrac{1}{2}$	0	-1
$\tan\theta$	0	$\dfrac{1}{\sqrt{3}}$	1	$\sqrt{3}$	undefined	0

5.3 Plots of Trigonometric Functions

Sine Function

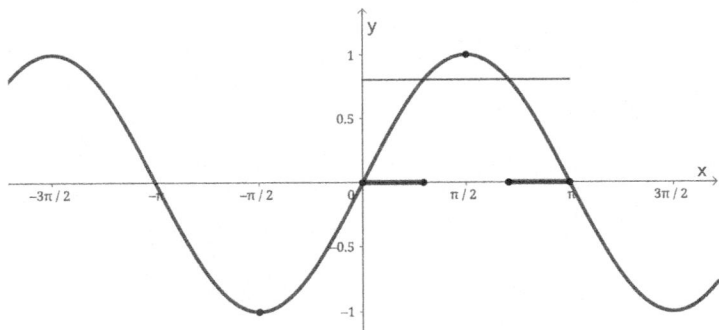

Figure 5.3: Interval where $\sin(x) \leq 0.8$ and $0 \leq x \leq \pi$

1. sin attains its maximum at $(4n+1)\frac{\pi}{2}$ and minimums at $(4n-1)\frac{\pi}{2}$

2. sin is convex on $[(2n-1)\pi, 2n\pi]$ and is concave on $[2n\pi, (2n+1)\pi]$

3. If we are trying to find $0 < \sin x < c$ on $[0, 2\pi]$, we only need to focus on $[0, \pi]$, and the region will be of the form $(0, t) \cup (\pi - t, \pi)$ for the unknown variable t.

Cosine Function

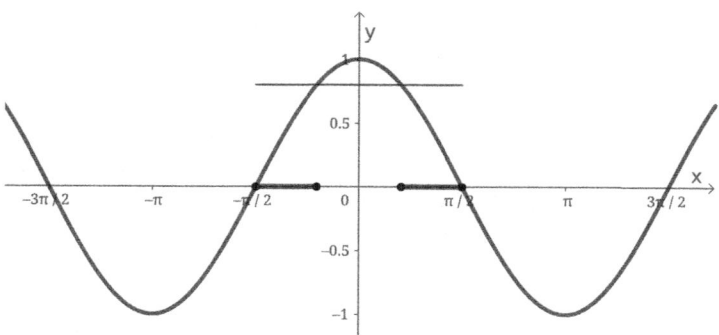

Figure 5.4: Interval where $\cos(x) \leq 0.8$ and $-\frac{\pi}{2} \leq x \leq \frac{\pi}{2}$

1. cos attains its maximums at $2n\pi$ and minimums at $(2n-1)\pi$

2. cos is convex on $[(4n+1)\frac{\pi}{2}, (4n+3)\frac{\pi}{2}]$ and is concave on $[(4n-1)\frac{\pi}{2}, (4n+1)\frac{\pi}{2}])$

3. If we are trying to find $0 < \cos x < c$ on $[-\pi, \pi]$, we only need to focus on $[-\frac{\pi}{2}, \frac{\pi}{2}]$, and the region will be of the form $(-\frac{\pi}{2}, -t) \cup (t, \pi)$ for the unknown variable t.

Tangent Function

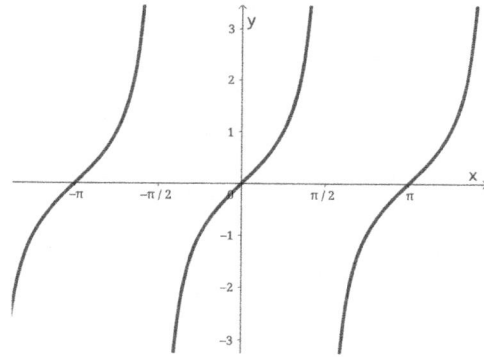

Figure 5.5: Tangent function

1. tan does not have a global maximum or minimum.

2. tan is convex on $[n\pi, n\pi + \frac{\pi}{2}]$ and concave on $[n\pi + \frac{\pi}{2}, (n+1)\pi]$

5.4 Solving equations

General techniques

1. If the equation involves both squares of sin and cos, use the Pythagorean identity to convert it into an equation only involving either sin or cos.

2. If the equation is a polynomial on $\sin x$, first solve for $\sin x$.

3. After finding all possible values of $\sin x$ (or $\cos x$), use the general solutions to $\sin x$.

4. Remember that $\sin x = c, \cos x = d$ has solutions only if $|c| \leq 1, |d| \leq 1$. $\tan x = c$ has solutions for all values of $c in \mathbb{R}$.

> **Example 5.1** (MAT 2015 Question 1.E). How many solutions does the following equation have on the interval $0 \leq x \leq 2\pi$?
>
> $$\sin(2\cos(2x) + 2) = 0$$

Solution. We know $\sin(y) = \sin 0$ has the solutions $y = -2\pi, -\pi, 0, \pi, 2\pi \ldots$.

But not all of these values will be relevant to us, because $2\cos(2x) + 2$ can only take values in $[0, 4]$. So, we can only check the values of $0, \pi$.

If $2\cos(2x) + 2 = 0$, then $\cos(2x) = -1 = \cos \pi$, so

$$2x = \pi, 3\pi, 5\pi, \text{ etc}$$

But for x to be in the interval $[0, 2\pi]$, we need $2x = \pi$ or 3π.

If $2\cos(2x) + 2 = \pi$, then $\cos(2x) = \frac{\pi}{2} - 1$.

Now $2x$ can take values in $[0, 4\pi]$. As $\cos(y) = \frac{\pi}{2} - 1$ has two solutions in both $[0, 2\pi]$ and $[2\pi, 4\pi]$, we find 4 solutions of x.

So in total, there are 6 solutions. □

Tips

1. When solving equations involving trigonometric functions, be aware of the interval on which the solution should lie.

2. Often, drawing the graphs of the function helps determine the solution regions.

3. Remember the identities while simplifying/solving an equation. Especially the formulas involving sum of angles and the Pythagorean formula involving sin and cos.

5.5 Walkthrough: MAT 2010 Question P3

Question

> In the diagram below OA and OC are of length 1 and subtend an angle x at O. The angle BAO is a right angle and the circular arc from A to C, centred at O, is also drawn.
>
> **Part i.** By consideration of various areas in the above diagram, show, for $0 < x < \frac{\pi}{2}$, that $x\cos x < \sin x < x$
>
> **Part ii.** Sketch the graph of
> $$y = \frac{\sin x}{x}, \quad 0 < x < 4\pi$$
> Justify your value that y takes as x becomes small.
>
> **Part iii.** Draw the graph of $y = \sin x$. Sketch the line $y = cx$ where $c > 0$ is such that the equation $\sin x = cx$ has exactly 5 solutions.
>
> **Part iv.** Draw the line $y = c$.
>
> **Part v.** If X is the largest of the five solutions of the equation $\sin x = cx$, explain why $\tan X = X$.

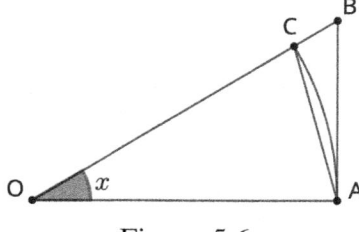

Figure 5.6

Solution

> (Part i) In the diagram below OA and OC are of length 1 and subtend an angle x at O. The angle BAO is a right angle and the circular arc from A to C, centred at O, is also drawn.
>
> By consideration of various areas in the above diagram, show, for $0 < x < \frac{\pi}{2}$, that
> $$x\cos x < \sin x < x$$

Solution. Let x denote the angle subtended by the two sides of length 1.

1. The area of the smaller triangle is $\frac{1}{2}\sin x$,
2. of the sector is $\frac{1}{2}x$, and,
3. of the larger triangle is $\frac{1}{2}\tan x$

So $\sin x < x < \tan x$. Multiplying the second inequality by $\cos x > 0$ (for $0 < x < \frac{\pi}{2}$) we have $x\cos x < \sin x < x$. □

> (Part ii) Sketch, on the axes provided on the opposite page, the graph of
> $$y = \frac{\sin x}{x}, \quad 0 < x < 4\pi$$
> Justify your value that y takes as x becomes small.

Solution. We have $\cos x < \frac{\sin x}{x} < 1$ for small values of x.

As $\cos x \approx 1$ for small values of x then $\sin x / x \approx 1$ for small values of 1.

The function $\frac{\sin x}{x}$ changes sign as $\sin x$, and grows smaller as x grows bigger. So the resulting graph is:

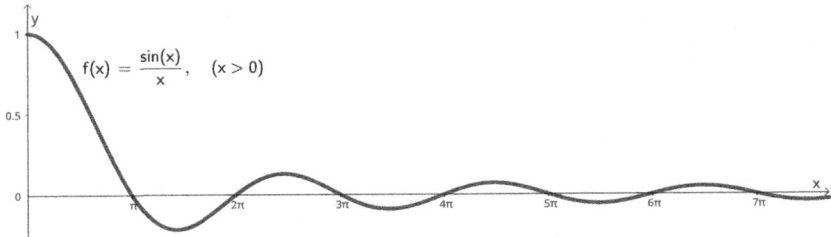

Figure 5.7

(Part iii) Drawn below is a graph of $y = \sin x$. Sketch the line $y = cx$ where $c > 0$ is such that the equation $\sin x = cx$ has exactly 5 solutions.

Solution. The line should be drawn so that it **passes through the origin** and is **tangential to the second hump** above the y-axis and likewise **tangential in the third quadrant**.

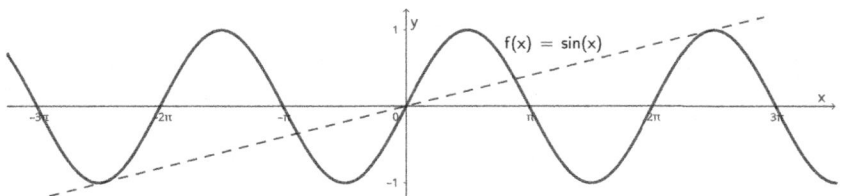

Figure 5.8

(Part iv) Draw the line $y = c$.

Solution. The line $y = c$ should be tangential with the second positive hump of the $y = \sin x / x$ graph.

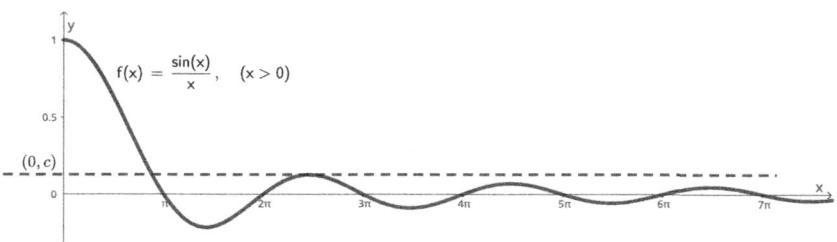

Figure 5.9

(Part v) If X is the largest of the five solutions of the equation $\sin x = cx$, explain why $\tan X = X$.

Solution. As X is a solution of $\sin x = cx$ then we have $\sin X = cX$.

But $y = cx$ is also tangential to $y = \sin x$ when $x = X$ and so the gradients also agree, i.e. $\cos X = c$.

Eliminating c and rearranging we get $\tan X = X$.

CHAPTER 6
Functions and Polynomials

6.1 Functions

A function from set A to set B is a mapping that maps the elements of A to some element in B according to some given rule. We write this as $f : A \to B$, a function from the set A to the set B. For example, $f : \mathbb{N} \to \mathbb{N}$ and $f(n) = n+1$ is a function from the natural numbers to the natural numbers given by the rule $f(n) = n+1$.

A well-defined function will map an element a in A to a unique element b in B, and it will do this for all the elements in A. In other words, when we write $f(a)$, we refer to the unique "image" of a in B under the function f.

Domain and Range

Suppose $f : A \to B$ is a function from the set A to the set B.

We call A the **domain** of f, the set of values that are allowed as inputs to f.

And we call B, the **range** of f, the set of values that the function can return as outputs.

For example, the function $f(x) = \frac{1}{x}$ is defined for all $x \in \mathbb{R}$ except for $x = 0$. And the output of the function will be any real number other than 0. So its domain and range are both $\mathbb{R} \setminus \{0\}$.

Note that we can restrict the domain and range of f here, and say $f : (1, 2] \to [\frac{1}{2}, 1)$.

We say that two functions $f : A \to B, g : A \to C$ are equal if their domains are the same, and **for all** $a \in A, f(a) = g(a)$.

The possible values that $f(a)$ might take in B are collectively called the **image** of f. More precisely

$$\text{image of } f = \{f(a) | a \in A\}$$

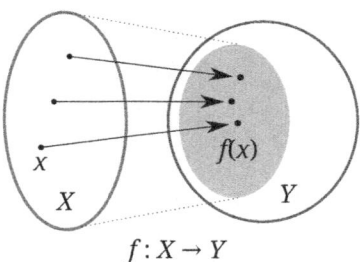

Figure 6.1: The shaded set is the image of f

Special functions

There are some functions that we are especially interested in. Suppose $f : A \to B$ is a function.

Onto If for every element $b \in B$, there is an $a \in A$ such that $f(a) = b$, then we call f an **onto** or **surjective** function.

If f is surjective, we necessarily have $|B| \leq |A|$.

1-1 If f maps different elements in A to different elements in B, that is, if for all $a_1, a_2 \in A$, $f(a_1) \neq f(a_2)$, then we call f a **one-to-one** or **injective** function.

If f is injective, we necessarily have $|A| \leq |B|$.

Bijection If f is onto and one-to-one, then we call it a **bijective** function, or simply a **bijection**.

If f is a bijection, we have $|A| = |B|$.

Monotonicity

Suppose $f : A \to B$ is a function. f is

increasing if for all $x, y \in A$ and $x < y$, $f(x) \leq f(y)$

decreasing if for all $x, y \in A$ and $x < y$, $f(x) \geq f(y)$

strictly increasing if for all $x, y \in A$ and $x < y$, $f(x) < f(y)$

strictly decreasing if for all $x, y \in A$ and $x < y$, $f(x) > f(y)$

If a function is either increasing or decreasing, we call it **monotonic**.

Function Composition

If $f : B \to C$ and $g : A \to B$ is a function, then $f \circ g$ is a function from A to C, and is defined by:
$$(f \circ g)(a) = f(g(a)), \text{ for all } a \in A$$

Note that, the outputs of g needs to be in the domain of f. So if for example, $f(x) = \frac{1}{x}$ and $g(x) = 2x - 1$, then $f \circ g$ is defined only when $2x - 1 \neq 0$, that is, the **domain of $f \circ g$ is** $\mathbb{R} \setminus \{\frac{1}{2}\}$.

Also note that $f \circ g \neq g \circ f$, and that even though $f \circ g$ is well-defined, $g \circ f$ might not be.

Tips

1. It is best to think of functions as a black box, that takes an input and spits out an output.

2. When deciding for the domain and range, think of when the function is well-defined.

6.2 Functional equations

Functional equations

Sometimes a question will give you the name of a function f, its domain and range, and an equation involving f that is satisfied for all inputs. The question will ask you to find all of the functions that satisfy these conditions.

For example, one such problem might ask: find all functions $f : \mathbb{Q} \to \mathbb{Q}$ that satisfies

$$f(x+y) = f(x) + f(y)$$

for all $x, y \in \mathbb{Q}$

To solve these problems, we need to manipulate the inputs in the equations.

Solving functional equations

Let us try to answer the previous question. We have $f : \mathbb{Q} \to \mathbb{Q}$, and f satisfies for all $x, y \in \mathbb{Q}$ the equation

$$f(x+y) = f(x) + f(y)$$

We begin by plugging in values of x, y into the equation.

1. $x = 0, y = 0$: $f(0) = 2f(0) \implies f(0) = 0$

2. $y = -x$: $f(0) = f(x) + f(-x) \implies f(x) = -f(-x)$

3. $x = 1, y = 1$: $f(2) = 2f(1)$

4. $x = 2, y = 1$: $f(3) = 3f(1)$

5. $x = 1, y = -1$: $f(-1) = -f(1)$

6. $x = -1, y = -1$: $f(-2) = -2f(1)$

This makes us hypothesise that $f(n) = nf(1)$ for all $n \in \mathbb{Z}$. We can easily prove this by induction:

$$f(n) = nf(1) \implies \begin{cases} f(n+1) = f(n) + f(1) = (n+1)f(1) \\ f(n-1) = f(n) - f(1) = (n-1)f(1) \end{cases}$$

This is easily extended to $f(nx) = nf(x)$, by replacing 1 by x.

Now we've found the values of f at the integers. What about the non-integer rational numbers?

Suppose $x = \frac{p}{q}$ is a rational number, where p, q are integers. We know

$$f(qx) = qf(x)$$
$$\implies qf(x) = f(p) = pf(1)$$
$$\implies f(x) = \frac{p}{q}f(1)$$

So we have showed that for all rational number p, q, $f\left(\frac{p}{q}\right) = \frac{p}{q}f(1)$, which is the general solution to the given functional equation.

Tips

1. The best way to get started with a functional equation is to plug in values like $0, 1, -1$ etc.

2. If you find any interesting equations, try to reuse them.

3. In questions involving repeated function composition, induction might be a very useful tool.

4. In recursive functions, remember that the recursion is defined for all values of n. For example, if f is defined by $f(2n) = f(n) + 1$ and $f(2n+1) = 2f(n-1)$, for all n, then while evaluating $f(10)$, you can repeatedly use this recursion.

6.3 Walkthrough: MAT 2007 Question 2

Question

Let $f_n(x) = (2+(-2)^n)x^2 + (n+3)x + n^2$ where n is a positive integer and x is a real number.

Part i. Write down $f_3(x)$. Find the maximum value of $f_3(x)$. For what values of n does $f_n(x)$ have a maximum value (as x varies)?

Part ii. Write down $f_1(x)$ and calculate $f_1(f_1(x))$ and $f_1(f_1(f_1(x)))$.

Find an expression, simplified as much as possible, for

$$f_1(f_1(f_1(\cdots f_1(x))))$$

where f_1 is applied k times. [Here k is a positive integer.]

Part iii. Write down $f_2(x)$.

The function

$$f_2(f_2(f_2(\cdots f_2(x)))),$$

where f_2 is applied k times, is a polynomial in x. What is the degree of this polynomial?

Solution

(Part i) Write down $f_3(x)$. Find the maximum value of $f_3(x)$. For what values of n does $f_n(x)$ have a maximum value (as x varies)?

Solution. Setting $n=3$ in the definition of $f_n(x)$, we have,

$$f_3(x) = -6x^2 + 6x + 9 = -6\left(x^2 - x - \frac{3}{2}\right)$$

$$= -6\left(\left(x-\frac{1}{2}\right)^2 - \frac{7}{4}\right) = -6\left(x-\frac{1}{2}\right)^2 + \frac{21}{2}$$

We have,

$$f_3(x) = -6\left(x-\frac{1}{2}\right)^2 + \frac{21}{2}$$

Now, notice that $\left(x-\frac{1}{2}\right)^2 \geq 0$, and hence $-6\left(x-\frac{1}{2}\right)^2 \leq 0$. So the maximum value this can achieve is 0 which is achieved at $x = \frac{1}{2}$.

6.3. WALKTHROUGH: MAT 2007 QUESTION 2

Hence, the maximum value of $f_3(x)$ is $\frac{21}{2} = 10.5$ and it is achieved at $x = \frac{1}{2}$.

For any n, $f_n(x)$ is a quadratic function in x which has a maximum only when the lead coefficient is negative (the function is upside down). For that we need $2 + (-2)^n < 0$. This is achieved when n is an odd number greater than 1. $\square$

> (Part ii) Write down $f_1(x)$ and calculate $f_1(f_1(x))$ and $f_1(f_1(f_1(x)))$.
>
> Find an expression, simplified as much as possible, for
>
> $$f_1(f_1(f_1(\cdots f_1(x))))$$
>
> where f_1 is applied k times. [Here k is a positive integer.]

Solution. Setting $n = 1$ in the given equation, we have $f_1(x) = 4x + 1$. Plugging in $f_1(x)$ inside f_1 we get,

$$f_1(f_1(x)) = 4(4x + 1) + 1 = 16x + 5$$

Again, pluggin in $f_1(x)$ in $f_1(f_1(x))$, we get,

$$f_1(f_1(f_1(x))) = 4(16x + 5) + 1 = 64x + 21$$

We see a pattern: the coefficient of x is 4^k and the constant term is $1 + 4 + 16 + \ldots 4^{k-1}$.

So we try to prove this by induction on the value of k. The base case is immediate as for $k = 1$, $f_1(x) = 4^1 + 4^0$.

Now, let $f_1^k(x) = 4^k x + (1 + 4 + \cdots + 4^{k-1})$ for some k. Then,

$$\begin{aligned} f_1^{k+1}(x) &= f_1^k(f_1(x)) \\ &= 4^k(f_1(x)) + (1 + 4 + \cdots + 4^{k-1}) \\ &= 4^k(4x + 1) + (1 + 4 + \cdots + 4^{k-1}) \\ &= 4^{k+1}x + (1 + 4 + \cdots + 4^{k-1} + 4^k) \end{aligned}$$

Therefore by induction, $f_1^k(x) = 4^k x + (1 + 4 + \cdots + 4^{k-1}) = 4^k x + \frac{1}{3}(4^k - 1)$ for all natural number k. $\square$

> (Part iii) Write down $f_2(x)$.
>
> The function
>
> $$f_2(f_2(f_2(\cdots f_2(x)))),$$
>
> where f_2 is applied k times, is a polynomial in x. What is the degree of this polynomial?

Solution. Setting $n = 2$ we have $f_2(x) = 6x^2 + 5x + 4$. $f_2(x)$ has degree 2.

When we plug $f_2(x)$ in f_2, the degree of x becomes double. Similarly, if we plug in a polynomial $P(x)$ of degree n, the degree of $f_2(P(x))$ will be $2n$. So by induction on k, we can show that $f_2^k(x)$ will be a polynomial of degree 2^k. $\square$

6.4 Polynomials

Polynomials are a special kind of function from the real numbers to the real numbers, that have the form

$$P(x) = a_n x^n + a_{n-1} x^{n-1} \cdots + a_1 x + a_0$$

where $a_n, a_{n-1}, \ldots, a_0$ are real numbers called "coefficients".

We require $a_n \neq 0$ so that the polynomial has a definite **degree**: the greatest number n such that the coefficient of x^n in P is non-zero. We write,

$$\deg(P) = n$$

Note that all the other coefficients can be 0.

Equality of polynomials

If two polynomials

$$P(x) = a_n x^n + \cdots + a_0 \text{ and } Q(x) = b_m x^m + \ldots b_0$$

are equal, that is, for all real number x, $P(x) = Q(x)$, then

1. The degrees of P and Q are equal, that is, $n = m$

2. The respective coefficients are all equal, that is, for all $i = 0, 1, \ldots n$,

$$a_i = b_i$$

So when equating polynomials, we can compare them by their coefficients.

Order of growth

Informally speaking, we say that f is a faster growing function than g, where $f, g : \mathbb{R} \to \mathbb{R}$ are real valued functions, if for all "large enough" values of x, $f(x) \geq g(x)$.

For example, x^2 grows faster than $x+2$, as if you plot these two functions on a graph, at some point x^2 crosses $x+2$. Similarly x^3 grows faster than $5x^2$, as for all $x > 5$, $f(x) > g(x)$.

Now, with polynomials, we can intuit that if $P(x)$ has a greater degree than $Q(x)$, then $P(x)$ grows faster than $Q(x)$. Which is precisely the case, and is captured by the following theorem.

> **Theorem 6.1** (Order of growth for polynomials) — Let $P(x)$ be a polynomial with degree n. Then x^{n+1} grows faster than $P(x)$.

Hopefully you can see why this is true without requiring a rigorous argument: if x is very large, then $x \times x^n$ will be much larger than $a_n \times x^n$, and for the rest of the terms as well. We can make this argument a lot more precise, however.

Proof. Let $P(x) = a_n x^n + a_{n-1} x^{n-1} \cdots + a_1 x + a_0$, and let $M = \max\{|a_n|, \ldots |a_1|, |a_0|\}$. The for all $x > M(n+1)$, we have

$$x > (n+1)|a_k| \text{ for all } k \text{ and } x^{n+1} > (n+1)|a_k| x^k \geq a_k x^k$$

Hence, summing up for $k = 0, \ldots n$, we have

$$(n+1)x^{n+1} > (n+1)P(x) \implies x^{n+1} > P(x) \text{ for all } x > M(n+1)$$

$\square$

Roots of Polynomials

If a number (either real or complex) x satisfies $P(x) = 0$, then we call that a **root** of P.

> **Theorem 6.2** (Fundamental theorem of algebra) — Every non-constant polynomial has **at least one complex root**. Therefore, as an extension, we know that every polynomial with degree n has at most n complex roots.

Note that the theorem only guarantees the existence of complex roots. Whether a polynomial has a real root is difficult to determine.

Interpretation of real roots

If α is a real root of the polynomial P, then if we sketch the graph of $P(x)$ in an xy-plane, the graph will intersect with the x axis at $(\alpha, 0)$.

Using this intuition, we have this theorem.

> **Theorem 6.3** (Intermediate Value Theorem) — If there are $a, b \in \mathbb{R}$ such that $P(a) < 0$ and $P(b) > 0$, then there exists a real root of P between a and b.

A direct application of this theorem is the theorem about the existence of a real root of odd degree polynomials.

> **Theorem 6.4** (Real root of odd degree polynomials) — A polynomial $P(x)$ with degree n where n is an odd number always has at least one real root.

Proof. Let $P(x) = a_n x^n + \ldots a_1 x + a_0$, where n is odd. Using the concept of order of growth, we see that $a_n x^n$ grows faster than $Q(x) = a_{n-1} x^{n-1} + \cdots + a_1 x + a_0$, or in other words, in $P(x)$, the term $a_n x^n$ "dominates".

Let's consider the case $a_n > 0$. The other case follows similarly. Writing $P(x) = a_n x^n + Q(x)$, notice that even if $Q(x)$ is negative, for large x, $a_n x^n$ will be greater than $Q(x)$ or $|Q(x)|$. So overall $P(x)$ will be positive.

Similarly, for negative enough x, even if $Q(x)$ is positive, since x^n dominates, overall $P(x)$ will be negative, so there will always be two points a, b such that $P(a) < 0, P(b) > 0$. So by the Intermediate Value Theorem, there will always be a real root of P if the degree of P is odd. □

Remark. Can you see the problem with even-degree polynomials, and why we can't guarantee that there will always be a real root of an even-degree polynomial?

Can you answer why there will always be an even number of real roots for an even-degree polynomial and an odd number of real roots for an odd-degree polynomial?

Double root

A root r of $P(x)$ is called a "double root" if r is also a root of $P'(x)$. If r is a double root of P, then $(x-r)^2$ divides $P(x)$, or the exponent of $(x-r)$ in the factorisation of $P(x)$ is at least 2. When plotting a function (a double root can also exist for general functions) with a double

6.4. POLYNOMIALS

root, the curve of the function around the root looks flatter.

Quadratic polynomials

We call polynomials with degree 2, **quadratic polynomials**. A general quadratic polynomial has the form
$$P(x) = ax^2 + bx + c$$
where $a \neq 0$. Unlike polynomials of a much higher degree, we can say for sure when a quadratic polynomial has solutions.

> **Theorem 6.5** (Solution to quadratic polynomials) — For the quadratic polynomial above, define the "determinant" to be $D = b^2 - 4ac$.
>
> 1. If $D > 0$, then there are two distinct roots of $P(x)$
> 2. If $D = 0$, then there is an unique root of $P(x)$
> 3. If $D < 0$, then both roots of P are complex.

Graph of Quadratic Polynomials

We can infer important information about the roots of a quadratic polynomial from its graph:

1. If P has two distinct real roots, the graph of P intersect x axis at two different points.
2. If P has an unique real root, the graph of P touches the x axis at the root.
3. If P has no real root, that is, both of its roots are complex, the graph of P does not intersect the x axis.

> **Example 6.1** (MAT 2013 Question 1.A). For what values of the real number a does the quadratic equation
> $$x^2 + ax + a = 1$$
> have distinct real roots?

Solution. Rewrite the equation as a polynomial
$$P(x) = x^2 + ax + (a-1)$$

So we are interested in the roots of P.

We know P has distinct real roots if the determinant of P is greater than 0.

We have the determinant of P

$$D = a^2 - 4(a-1) = a^2 - 4a + 4 = (a-2)^2$$

So $D \geq 0$ for all values of a, but $D = 0$ if $a = 2$. So $D > 0$ for all values of $a \neq 2$. □

Tips

1. In problems related to solving equations with terms like x^k, convert the equation into a root-finding question for polynomials.

2. Be careful with the three cases of the determinants of a quadratic polynomial.

6.5 Factorisation

Euclidean Division of Polynomials

Just like integer division, we can use long division in polynomials:

> **Theorem 6.6** (Euclidean Division) — Suppose P, Q are polynomials such that the degree of P is greater or equal than the degree of Q. Then we can find unique polynomials S, R such that R **has degree less than the degree of** Q and
>
> $$P(x) = Q(x)S(x) + R(x) \text{ for all } x \in \mathbb{R}$$

Just like integers, we say $Q(x)$ divides $P(x)$ if $R(x) = 0$.

Remainder Theorem

If we take $Q(x) = x - a$ for real number a in the Euclidean Division theorem, we see that R must be a constant polynomial.

Note that, $Q(a) = 0$. So we have $P(a) = R(a)$, which gives us the Remainder theorem –

6.5. FACTORISATION

> **Theorem 6.7** (Remainder Theorem) — The remainder of P upon division by $(x-a)$ is $P(a)$.

As a corollary to this theorem, we have –

> **Theorem 6.8** (Factor Theorem) — $(x-a)$ is a divisor of $P(x)$ if and only $P(a) = 0$, that is, a is a root of P.

Example 6.2 (MAT 2013 Question 1.G). Let $n \geqslant 2$ be an integer and $p_n(x)$ be the polynomial
$$p_n(x) = (x-1) + (x-2) + \cdots + (x-n)$$
What is the remainder when $p_n(x)$ is divided by $p_{n-1}(x)$?

Solution. The polynomial p_n is actually a one degree polynomial, which can be simplified as:
$$p_n(x) = nx - \frac{n(n+1)}{2}$$

As the degrees of p_n and p_{n-1} are equal, we know by the Euclidean division theorem, there are constants c, d such that
$$p_n(x) = cp_{n-1}(x) + d \text{ for all } x \in \mathbb{R}$$

We are only interested in the constant term d. Expanding the terms gives us
$$nx - \frac{1}{2}n(n+1) = c(n-1)x - \frac{1}{2}cn(n-1) + d$$

Equating the terms, we must have
$$n = c(n-1) \text{ and } \frac{1}{2}n(n+1) = \frac{1}{2}cn(n-1) - d$$

Solving for c, d gives us
$$c = \frac{n}{n-1} \text{ and } d = -\frac{n}{2}$$

$\square$

Extending the idea from the factor theorem, we get:

Theorem 6.9 (Unique Factorisation of a polynomial) — If $P(x) = a_n x^n + a_{n-1} x^{n-1} + \ldots a_1 x + a_0$ has roots $r_1, r_2, \ldots r_n$, either real or complex, then the following equation holds:
$$P(x) = a_n(x - r_1)(x - r_2) \ldots (x - r_n)$$

Thus, every polynomial of degree n can be written as the product of n one degree polynomials.

Factorisation Identities

The following identities are useful in many situations, not just in polynomials:

1. $x^2 - y^2 = (x+y)(x-y)$, common situations in polynomials arise when y is a constant, or is another polynomial.

2. $x^n - y^n = (x-y)\left(x^{n-1} + x^{n-2}y + \ldots xy^{n-2} + y^{n-1}\right)$ common situations involve y as a constant, specially 1.

3. $x^n + y^n = (x+y)\left(x^{n-1} - x^{n-2}y + x^{n-3}y^2 + \cdots + (-1)^{n-1}y^{n-1}\right)$ for odd n.

Example 6.3 (MAT 2019 Question 1.C). For which values of the constant c, the equation $x^4 = (x-c)^2$ has four real solutions?

Solution. We bring everything to one side and factorise
$$x^4 - (x-c)^2 = (x^2 - x + c)(x^2 + x - c) = 0$$

As we need 4 roots, we must have $x^2 - x + c = 0$ and $x^2 + x - c = 0$.

Solving for the first polynomial tells us that we need
$$D_1 = 1^2 - 4c \geq 0 \implies c \leq \frac{1}{4}$$

And the second polynomial tells us
$$D_2 = 1 + 4c \geq 0 \implies c \geq -\frac{1}{4}$$

Putting these together, we have
$$-\frac{1}{4} \leq c \leq \frac{1}{4}$$

□

6.5. FACTORISATION

Root-coefficient relation

Continuing from our last theorem, it tells us that

$$a_n(x-r_1)(x-r_2)\ldots(x-r_n) = a_n x^n + a_{n-1} x^{n-1} + \ldots a_1 x + a_0$$

for all $x \in \mathbb{R}$.

Now dividing both sides by a_n, we get

$$(x-r_1)(x-r_2)\ldots(x-r_n) = x^n + \frac{a_{n-1}}{a_n} x^{n-1} + \ldots \frac{a_1}{a_n} x + \frac{a_0}{a_n}$$

If we expand the left hand side of the equation, and equate the coefficients on both sides, we get a set of equations which are collectively known as Vieta's formulas.

Vieta's Formulas

If for all $x \in \mathbb{R}$,

$$(x-r_1)(x-r_2)\ldots(x-r_n) = x^n + \frac{a_{n-1}}{a_n} x^{n-1} + \ldots \frac{a_1}{a_n} x + \frac{a_0}{a_n}$$

Then the following equations hold:

$$r_1 + r_2 + \cdots + r_n = (-1)^1 \frac{a_{n-1}}{a_n}$$

$$r_1 r_2 + r_1 r_3 + \cdots + r_{n-1} r_n = (-1)^2 \frac{a_{n-2}}{a_n}$$

$$\vdots$$

$$r_1 r_2 \ldots r_n = (-1)^n \frac{a_0}{a_n}$$

6.6 Walkthrough, Specimen B Question 2

Question

Suppose that the equation

$$x^4 + Ax^2 + B = (x^2 + ax + b)(x^2 - ax + b)$$

holds for all values of x.

Part i. Find A and B in terms of a and b.

Part ii. Use this information to find a factorisation of the expression

$$x^4 - 20x^2 + 16$$

as a product of two quadratics in x.

Part iii. Show that the four solutions of the equation

$$x^4 - 20x^2 + 16 = 0$$

can be written as $\pm\sqrt{7} \pm \sqrt{3}$

Solution

(Part i) Find A and B in terms of a and b.

Solution. We have an equality of polynomials, so we need to equate all the coefficients. We first expand the right hand side

$$\begin{aligned}&(x^2 + ax + b)(x^2 - ax + b) \\ &= x^4 + (a-a)x^3 + (b+b-a^2)x^2 + (-ab-ab)x + b^2 \\ &= x^4 + (2b - a^2)x^2 + b^2\end{aligned}$$

Now, equating the coefficients on both sides of the equation

$$x^4 + Ax^2 + B = x^4 + (2b - a^2)x^2 + b^2$$

we get, $A = 2b - a^2$, and $B = b^2$. □

> (Part.ii) Use this information to find a factorisation of the expression
> $$x^4 - 20x^2 + 16$$
> as a product of two quadratics in x.

Solution. We want to frame the coefficients of the given expression as in Part i. That is, we want to write
$$\left(x^2 + ax + b\right)\left(x^2 - ax + b\right) = x^4 - 20x^2 + 16$$
So we need to solve: $2b - a^2 = -20$ and $b^2 = 16$

These equations are solved by $b = 4$ and $a = \sqrt{28} = 2\sqrt{7}$. So
$$x^4 - 20x^2 + 16 = \left(x^2 - 2\sqrt{7}x + 4\right)\left(x^2 + 2\sqrt{7}x + 4\right)$$

Which is the product of two quadratics in x. □

> (Part iii) Show that the four solutions of the equation
> $$x^4 - 20x^2 + 16 = 0$$
> can be written as $\pm\sqrt{7} \pm \sqrt{3}$

Solution. By part ii, we get
$$x^4 - 20x^2 + 16 = \left(x^2 - 2\sqrt{7}x + 4\right)\left(x^2 + 2\sqrt{7}x + 4\right)$$

We want to find solutions to these two quadratic equations.

Finding the roots of these two quadratics we get
$$x^2 - 2\sqrt{7}x + 4 = 0$$
$$\implies (x - \sqrt{7})^2 = (\sqrt{7})^2 - 4 = 3$$
$$\implies x = \sqrt{7} \pm \sqrt{3}$$

and
$$x^2 + 2\sqrt{7}x + 4 = 0$$
$$\implies (x + \sqrt{7})^2 = (\sqrt{7})^2 - 4 = 3$$
$$\implies x = -\sqrt{7} \pm \sqrt{3}$$

Hence the four roots of $x^4 - 20x^2 + 16$ are $\pm\sqrt{7} \pm \sqrt{3}$. □

6.7 Common traps

1. Be careful about the sign of coefficients while using Vieta's formulas or equating coefficients to equate polynomials.

2. Be mindful of questions asking for specific roots of a polynomial, such as positive or distinct roots.

3. Turning points are easy to recognise and distinguish for polynomials, so keep these in mind while working with polynomials.

CHAPTER 7

Differentiation

7.1 Definition

Let $f : \mathbb{R} \to \mathbb{R}$ be a function from the real numbers to the real numbers. f is said to be **differentiable** at a point $a \in \mathbb{R}$ if the limit $\lim_{b \to a} \frac{f(b)-f(a)}{b-a}$ exists. In that case, the derivative of f at a is defined to be

$$\frac{\mathrm{d}f}{\mathrm{d}x}(a) = f'(a) = \lim_{b \to a} \frac{f(b)-f(a)}{b-a}$$

We can rewrite the limit as:

$$\frac{\mathrm{d}f}{\mathrm{d}x}(a) = f'(a) = \lim_{h \to 0} \frac{f(a+h)-f(a)}{h}$$

What this means is, the derivative of f at a is the limit of the gradients of the line passing through $A = (a, f(a))$ and $B = (b, f(b))$ as b moves closer to a.

For example, say we have a point $X = (a, f(a))$ on the graph. Let us slide a point $P = (b, f(b))$ on the graph towards X. As P gets closer to X, the line XP approaches the tangent to the graph at X.

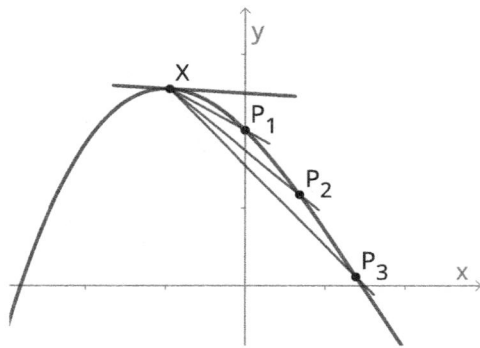

Figure 7.1: As P goes closer to X, the line XP goes towards the tangent at X

Note that the gradient of the line XP is

$$\frac{f(b)-f(a)}{b-a}$$

Since this gradient becomes the gradient of the tangent as P moves towards X, we can interpret the first derivative of f at a as the gradient of tangent line to f at point $(a, f(a))$.

7.1. DEFINITION

Caveats

Don't assume that every function will be differentiable or have a derivative. For example, the following function has no derivative at 0, that is, it's not differentiable at 0

$$f(x) = \begin{cases} -1 & \text{if } x < 0 \\ 1 & \text{if } x \geq 0 \end{cases}$$

That's because there's a "discontinuity" of the graph on that point.

Fortunately, on MAT, you won't be asked questions about functions that are not differentiable. But do be careful about this caveat if you wish to use differentiation in some unconventional setting where the underlying function is not well-behaved.

Differentiation Rules

If f, g are two functions that are differentiable, we have,

Addition Rule $(f+g)' = f' + g'$

Multiplication Rule $(fg)' = gf' + fg'$. Especially, for all constant λ, $(\lambda f)' = \lambda f'$

Division Rule $\left(\dfrac{f}{g}\right)' = \dfrac{gf' - fg'}{g^2}$. Especially if $f(x) = 1$, $\left(\dfrac{1}{g}\right)' = -\dfrac{g'}{g^2}$

Chain Rule $f(g(x))' = f'(g(x)) \times g'(x)$, or more concisely, $(f \circ g)' = (f' \circ g)g'$

For example, if we want to differentiate the function $\sin(x^2)$, we use chain rule as follows:

$$\frac{d}{dx}\sin(x^2) = \cos(x^2) \cdot \frac{d}{dx}x^2 = 2x\cos x$$

Derivatives of basic functions

Here, n means an integer, c is a constant

1. $\frac{d}{dx} c = 0$
2. $\frac{d}{dx} x^n = nx^{n-1}$
3. $\frac{d}{dx} e^x = e^x$
4. $\frac{d}{dx} \ln x = \frac{1}{x}$
5. $\frac{d}{dx} \sin x = \cos x$
6. $\frac{d}{dx} \cos x = \sin x$

Using the basic derivatives, we can derive the derivatives of more complicated functions. For example

1. $\frac{d}{dx} e^{cx} = ce^{cx}$

2. $\frac{d}{dx} \tan x = \frac{1}{\cos^2 x} = \sec^2 x$

3. $\frac{d}{dx} \log_a x = \frac{1}{x \ln a}$

While deriving more complicated functions, write the function in terms of addition, multiplication and composition of simpler functions, and then methodically apply the rules for differentiation.

> **Example 7.1.** Differentiate the function
> $$f(x) = e^{4x+\sin x} - 3x^5 \ln(x)$$

Solution. We can use addition rule to see,

$$f'(x) = \frac{d}{dx}\left(e^{4x+\sin x}\right) - \frac{d}{dx}\left(3x^5 \ln(x)\right)$$

To derive $e^{4x+\sin x}$, we note that this is a function composition with $g(x) = e^x$ and $h(x) = 4x + \sin x$, and by the chain rule, we have,

$$\frac{d}{dx} e^{4x+\sin x} = g(h(x))' = g'(h(x))h'(x) = e^{4x+\sin x}(4 + \cos x)$$

And by multiplication rule of differentiation, we have,

$$\frac{d}{dx}(3x^5 \ln x) = 15x^4 \ln x + 3x^5 \frac{1}{x} = 15x^4 \ln x + 3x^4$$

So the resulting derivative is $f'(x) = e^{4x+\sin x}(4 + \cos x) - 15x^4 \ln x - 3x^4$. □

Higher order derivatives

If we differentiate the first derivative of a function, we get the second derivative:

$$f''(x) = \frac{d}{dx} f'(x) = \frac{d^2}{dx^2} f$$

For example, if $f(x) = x^3$

$$f'(x) = 3x^2, f''(x) = 6x$$

Similarly we can define the higher order derivatives as follows:

$$f^{(3)} = f''' = (f'')', f^{(4)} = \left(f^{(3)}\right)', \ldots, f^{(n+1)} = \left(f^{(n)}\right)'$$

7.2 Monotonicity

We know, a function is **increasing** (respectively decreasing) if for all $x < y$, $f(x) \leq f(y)$ (respectively $f(x) \geq f(y)$)

And it is **strictly increasing** (respectively strictly decreasing) if for all $x < y$, $f(x) < f(y)$ (respectively $f(x) > f(y)$)

Derivatives help us determine whether a function is monotonic or not.

> **Theorem 7.1** (Monotonicity from derivatives) — Let f be a function, and f' be it's first derivative. We have,
>
> 1. f is **increasing** on $[a,b]$ if $f'(x) \geq 0$ for all $x \in [a,b]$
> 2. f is **strictly increasing** on $[a,b]$ if $f'(x) > 0$ for all $x \in [a,b]$
> 3. f is **decreasing** on $[a,b]$ if $f'(x) \leq 0$ for all $x \in [a,b]$
> 4. f is **strictly decreasing** on $[a,b]$ if $f'(x) < 0$ for all $x \in [a,b]$

For example, $f(x) = x^2$ is

1. Strictly increasing on $[0, \infty)$ as $f'(x) = 2x > 0$ for all $0 \in [0, \infty)$
2. Strictly decreasing on $(-\infty, 0]$ as $f'(x) = 2x < 0$ for all $0 \in (-\infty, 0]$

Graphical interpretation

Consider an arbitrary function that is differentiable at a. If $f'(a) > 0$ for some a, then the tangent at a to f is positively sloped. That means, around that point, the function is also increasing.

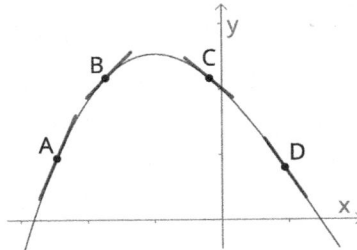

Figure 7.2: A, B have positive slope while C, D have negative slope

In the above graph, the tangents at A and B are positively sloped, and around those points, the function is also strictly increasing.

On the other hand, if $f'(a) < 0$, then the gradient is negatively sloped, and as a result, f is strictly decreasing around that point.

In the diagram, the gradients of f at C, D are negative, so f is decreasing around these points.

7.3 Turning Points

Turning points, also known as stationary points, are points on the graph of a function f where the f changes from being increasing to decreasing, or vice versa.

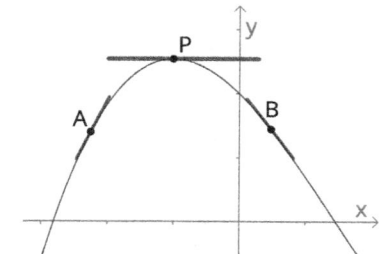

Figure 7.3: P is a turning point

In the above graph, P is the turning point, as the graph is increasing to the left of P and decreasing to the right of it.

Sufficient condition

We know a function is increasing when $f'(x) \geq 0$, and decreasing when $f'(x) \leq 0$. Since f changes from increasing to decreasing or vice versa at a turning point, its derivative changes sign at that point.

That's why if p is a turning point, then $f'(p) \geq 0$ and $f'(p) \leq 0$ at the same time, implying that $f'(p) = 0$. This means, the tangent to the curve of f at p is parallel to the x axis. This is known as Fermat's theorem.

So to find the turning points of a function, we first find the **roots of the function** $f'(x)$, that is, we solve the equation $f'(x) = 0$.

Categorising turning points

We categorise turning points based on whether the function change from being increasing to decreasing as well as from decreasing to increasing at that point.

1. If the function changes from **increasing to decreasing** at p, then we call p a **local maximum**. Here, P is a local maximum.

2. If the function changes from **decreasing to increasing** at p, then we call p a **local minimum**. Here, Q is a local minimum.

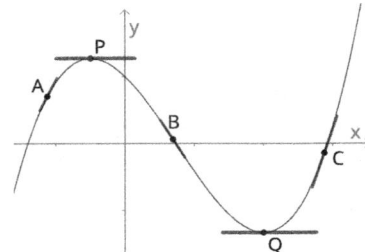

Figure 7.4: Local maximum at P, and local minimum at Q

Theorem 7.2 — By looking at the second derivative, we can categorise the turning points of a function f:

1. p is a local maximum if $f''(p) < 0$.

   Because f goes from increasing to decreasing at p, f' goes from positive to negative, hence **is decreasing**.

2. p is a local minimum if $f''(p) > 0$.

   Because f goes from decreasing to increasing at p, f' goes from negative to positive, hence **is increasing**.

Proof. We show the case for p being a maximum. The other case is analogous. Note that, at p, since it's a local maximum, the function first increases and then decreases. Hence, $f'(x) \geq 0$ for $x < p$ and $f'(x) \leq 0$ for $x > p$.

Also note that, as x approaches p from below, $f'(x)$ decreases till it becomes 0 at p. Similarly, as x goes further away from p, $f'(x)$ continues to decrease. This means, $f'(x)$ is strictly decreasing at p, which means $f''(p) < 0$. □

Inflection points

We've categorise the points where f' changes sign. But there might be other roots of f', where f' does not change sign. These points are called **inflection points**.

For example, consider $f(x) = x^3$, then $f'(x) = 3x^2$, which has a root at 0, but it does not change signs at 0. It is always non-negative. That's why 0 is neither a local maximum nor a local minimum of f.

Convexity

The shapes of $\cup$ and $\cap$ shapes in the curve of a function have mathematical meaning.

1. f is **convex** on $[a,b]$ if $f''(x) \geq 0$ for all $x \in [a,b]$.

2. f is **concave** on $[a,b]$ if $f''(x) \leq 0$ for all $x \in [a,b]$.

A convex function looks like a cup, and concave function looks like a hill.

Convex up, like a cup
Concave down, like a frown

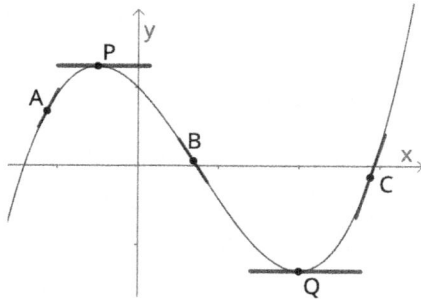

Figure 7.5: A function that is concave on one interval and convex on the other

In the above diagram, B is an inflection point, and the function is concave on the left of B and convex on the right of B.

Theorem 7.3 — A function changes from being convex to concave or vice-versa at an inflection point.

Caution

1. Be careful of the sign of $f''(x)$ when determining local maximum or local minimum. If you forget the correct condition, draw a diagram and figure out whether $f''(x)$ needs to be positive or negative.

2. $f''(x) \geq 0$ implies the turning point is a local minimum, and it also means the function is concave around that point.

3. $f''(x) \leq 0$ implies the turning point is a local maxima, and it also means the function is convex around that point.

7.4 Walkthrough: MAT Specimen B Question 3

Question

Let
$$f(x) = \begin{cases} x+1 & \text{for } 0 \leq x \leq 1 \\ 2x^2 - 6x + 6 & \text{for } 1 \leq x \leq 2 \end{cases}$$

Part i. Sketch a graph of $y = f(x)$ for $0 \leqslant x \leqslant 2$, labelling any turning points and the values attained at $x = 0, 1, 2$.

Part ii. For $1 \leqslant t \leqslant 2$, define
$$g(t) = \int_{t-1}^{t} f(x)\,dx$$

Express $g(t)$ as a cubic in t.

Part iii. Calculate and factorise $g'(t)$.

Part iv. What are the minimum and maximum values of $g(t)$ for t in the range $1 \leqslant t \leqslant 2$?

CHAPTER 7. DIFFERENTIATION

Solution

> (Part i) Sketch a graph of $y = f(x)$ for $0 \leqslant x \leqslant 2$, labelling any turning points and the values attained at $x = 0, 1, 2$.

Solution. After plotting the function, we notice that there's one local minima in the interval $(1, 2)$. To find this turning point, we need to differentiate the function $2x^2 - 6x + 6$ as this is the value f takes on this interval.

We note, on the interval $(1, 2)$, $f'(x) = 4x - 6 = 0$ when $x = 3/2$. Then

$$y = f\left(\frac{3}{2}\right) = 2\left(\frac{3}{2}\right)^2 - 6\left(\frac{3}{2}\right) + 6 = \frac{3}{2}$$

So the local minima is at the point $\left(\frac{3}{2}, \frac{3}{2}\right)$ □

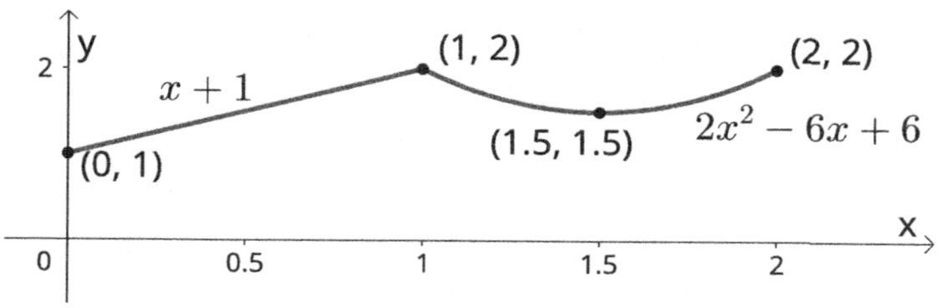

Figure 7.6

> (Part ii) For $1 \leqslant t \leqslant 2$, define
> $$g(t) = \int_{t-1}^{t} f(x) \, dx$$
> Express $g(t)$ as a cubic in t.

Solution. Splitting the integral of $f(x)$ about $x = 1$ we see

$$g(t) = \int_{t-1}^{1} (x+1) \, dx + \int_{1}^{t} 2x^2 - 6x + 6 \, dx$$

So,

$$g(t) = \left[\frac{(x+1)^2}{2}\right]_{t-1}^{1} + \left[\frac{2x^3}{3} - 3x^2 + 6x\right]_{1}^{t}$$

$$= \left(2 - \frac{t^2}{2}\right) + \left(\frac{2t^3}{3} - 3t^2 + 6t - \frac{2}{3} + 3 - 6\right)$$

$$\therefore g(t) = \frac{2t^3}{3} - \frac{7t^2}{2} + 6t - \frac{5}{3}$$

> (Part iii) Calculate and factorize $g'(t)$.

Solution. We have, $g'(t) = 2t^2 - 7t + 6 = (2t-3)(t-2)$.

> (Part iv) What are the minimum and maximum values of $g(t)$ for t in the range $1 \leqslant t \leqslant 2$?

Solution. The two turning points of g are $\frac{3}{2}$ and 2. Since the minimum/maximum might occur at the endpoints on the interval, the possible points for the minimum/maximum are $1, \frac{3}{2}$ or 2.

Note that
$$g(1) = \frac{2}{3} - \frac{7}{2} + 6 - \frac{5}{3} = \frac{3}{2}$$
$$g(2) = \frac{16}{3} - 14 + 12 - \frac{5}{3} = \frac{16 - 6 - 5}{3} = \frac{5}{3}$$

And,
$$g\left(\frac{3}{2}\right) = \frac{9}{4} - \frac{63}{8} + 9 - \frac{5}{3}$$
$$= \frac{9}{4} + \frac{9}{8} - \frac{5}{3} = \frac{54 + 27 - 40}{24} = \frac{41}{24};$$

These answers are respectively $\frac{36}{24}, \frac{40}{24}$ and $\frac{41}{24}$, the minimum of which is $\frac{36}{24}$ and the maximum of which is $\frac{41}{24}$.

Hence the minimum is at $t = 1$ and the maximum at $t = \frac{3}{2}$.

7.5 Common traps

1. While minimising (or maximising) a function on a closed interval, don't forget that the minimum (or maximum) might occur at the endpoints of the function.

2. Be careful about the signs when applying the division rule in differentiation.

3. Don't forget the $g'(x)$ part in chain rule.

4. Be careful about the inequality signs when determining turning points.

CHAPTER 8

Integration

8.1 Integration as area

Suppose $f : \mathbb{R} \to \mathbb{R}$ is a function. We define the **integral** of f between points a, b by the area enclosed by the curve of the function, the x axis, and the two lines $x = a$ and $x = b$:

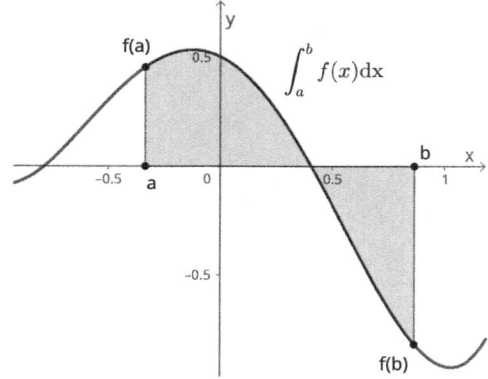

Figure 8.1: Integral of $f(x)$ between two points a, b

We could also say, "integral is the area under the curve between two points a, b". But strictly speaking, that wouldn't be true, as if f is negative, then the integral of f is thought to be the area above f and between the x axis.

The integral is written as $\int_a^b f(x)\mathrm{d}x$.

Since the area between the curve and the x axis between a to b is the sum of the area between a to c and from c to b, we have

$$\int_a^b f(x)\mathrm{d}x = \int_a^c f(x)\mathrm{d}x + \int_c^b f(x)\mathrm{d}x$$

for all $c \in (a, b)$.

Signed area

In the graph above, let c be the point where the graph intersects the x-axis. Since the area on the left side of c is above the x axis, the area is positive, and since the area on the right side of c is below the x axis, it is negative.

If f is a function that takes positive values on (a, b), then $\int_a^b f\mathrm{d}x > 0$, and if f takes negative values (a, b), then $\int_a^b f\mathrm{d}x < 0$.

Area between two curves

If f and g are two graphs, then we define the **area between f and g** between a, b as

$$A = \int_a^b (f(x) - g(x)) \mathrm{d}x = \int_a^b f(x) \mathrm{d}x - \int_a^b g(x) \mathrm{d}x$$

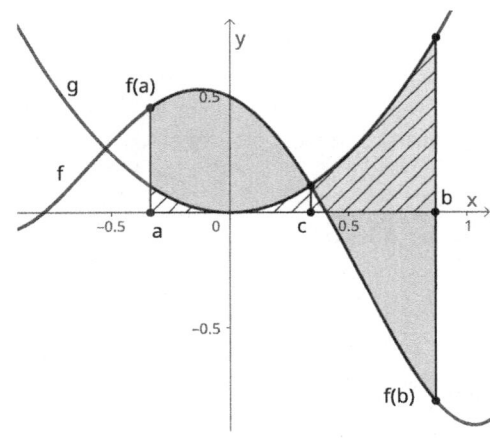

Figure 8.2

This is the area between the curves of the two functions and the two lines $x = a$ and $x = b$.

8.2 Trapezium Rule

We have so far discussed what the integral is. But how do we even calculate the integral of a given function? It is usually a tricky question to ask. Often, unlike differentiation, there doesn't exist a close form for integrals where we can plug in the values of a and b to get the integral. Most of the time we need to rely on approximation of the integral. Trapezium rule is one way to calculate the approximate value of the integral of a function.

With the trapezium rule, we approximate the integral of a function, and then keep refining our approximation until we reach close to the actual integral. The trapezium rule works by splitting the interval $[a, b]$ into n equal length parts. Then we approximate the area underneath the curve on each sub-interval by the trapezium formed by taking the two endpoints on the graph of the sub-interval. For example, consider the function from before:

In the first diagram, we divided the interval (a, b) into 4 sub-intervals, and in the second one we used 7 sub-intervals.

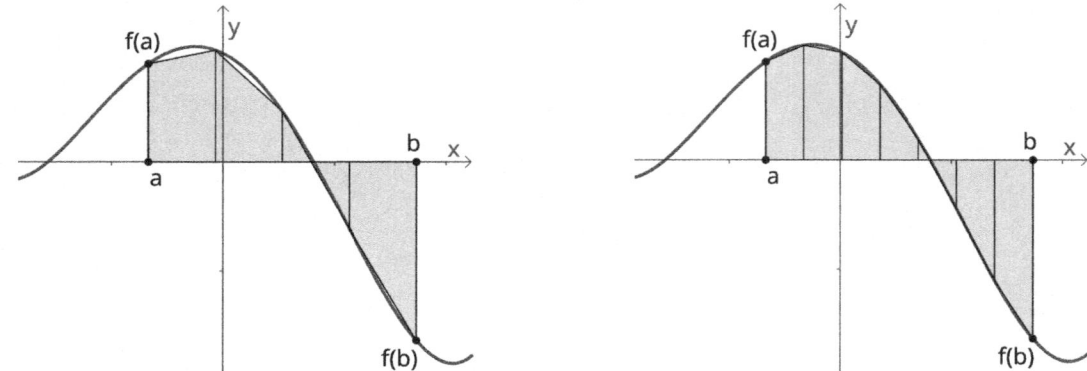

Figure 8.3: Approximating integral with Trapezium rule

If each sub-interval has length h, and the two endpoints are $d, d+h$, then the area of this trapezium is

$$\frac{1}{2}h(f(d)+f(d+h))$$

Now, we consider this area as an approximation to the actual area under the curve on the interval $(d, d+h)$. So to calculate the approximation of the integral between (a,b), we sum up the areas of the approximations on the sub-intervals.

So if we divide the interval $[a,b]$ into n subintervals with equal length, then we have $h = \frac{1}{n}(b-a)$ and our approximated integral is:

$$\int_a^b f(x)\,\mathrm{d}x \approx \frac{1}{2}h(f(a)+2f(a+h)+\ldots 2f(b-h)+f(b))$$

Another thing to notice here is that if we increase the value of n, the approximation gets progressively better. You can see this in the above diagram where the approximation with 7 sub-intervals is much better than the approximation with 4 intervals.

8.3 Indefinite Integration

If any of the endpoints in the definite integration is ∞ or $-\infty$, then we call the integration **indefinite**.

For example, $\int_1^\infty \frac{1}{x^2}dx = 1$. To calculate indefinite integrals, we express them as a limit of definite integrals:

$$\int_1^\infty \frac{1}{x^2}dx = \lim_{n\to\infty} \int_1^n \frac{1}{x^2}dx = \left[-\frac{1}{x}\right]_1^n = \lim_{n\to\infty}\left(1 - \frac{1}{n}\right) = 1$$

Indefinite Integration as the inverse of Differentiation

If $f(x)$ is a function that is sufficiently nice (more precisely, is differentiable and its derivative is integrable) and $f'(x) = \frac{d}{dx}f(x)$, then

$$f(x) = \int f'(x)dx + c$$

for some constant $c \in \mathbb{R}$.

This is known as the **Fundamental Theorem of Calculus**. Using this theorem, we can easily derive formulas for integration for some common functions. That is, if $f(x) = F'(x)$ for some $F(x)$, then $\int f dx = F(x)$.

Some common integration

$f(x)$	$\int f(x)$	$f(x)$	$\int f(x)$
$x^n, n \neq 1$	$\frac{1}{n+1}x^{n+1}$	$\sin kx$	$-\frac{1}{k}\cos x$
e^{ax+b}	$\frac{1}{a}e^{ax+b}$	$\cos x$	$\frac{1}{k}\sin x$
$\frac{1}{ax+b}$	$\frac{1}{a}\ln|ax+b|$	a^x	$\frac{1}{\ln a}a^x$

8.4 Walkthrough: MAT 2011 Question 3

Question

The graphs of $y = x^3 - x$ and $y = m(x - a)$ are drawn on the axes below. Here $m > 0$ and $a \leq -1$.

The line $y = m(x - a)$ meets the x-axis at $A = (a, 0)$, touches the cubic $y = x^3 - x$ at B and intersects again with the cubic at C. The x-coordinates of B and C are respectively b and c.

Part i Use the fact that the line and cubic touch when $x = b$, to show that $m = 3b^2 - 1$.

Part ii Show further that $a = \dfrac{2b^3}{3b^2 - 1}$

Part iii If $a = -10^6$, what is the approximate value of b ?

Part iv Using the fact that

$$x^3 - x - m(x - a) = (x - b)^2(x - c)$$

(which you need not prove), show that $c = -2b$.

Part v R is the finite region bounded above by the line $y = m(x - a)$ and bounded below by the cubic $y = x^3 - x$. For what value of a is the area of R largest?

Show that the largest possible area of R is $\frac{27}{4}$.

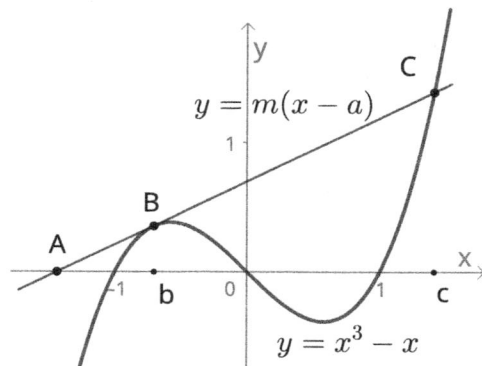

Figure 8.4

Solution

> (Part i) Use the fact that the line and cubic touch when $x = b$, to show that $m = 3b^2 - 1$.

Solution. The line with equation $y = m(x - a)$ touches the curve with equation $y = x^3 - x$ touch at $x = b$. That means, the gradient of the line is the same as the gradient of the curve at b.

The gradient of the line is m and the gradient of the tangent to the cubic at b is $3b^2 - 1$. Putting them together gives $m = 3b^2 - 1$. □

> (Part ii) Show further that
> $$a = \frac{2b^3}{3b^2 - 1}$$

Solution. As the line and the function intersect when $x = b$, the y-coordinates of the line and the graph at $x = b$ also agree.

So, $b^3 - b = m(b - a) = (3b^2 - 1)(b - a)$. Solving for a, we have

$$a = b - \left(\frac{b^3 - b}{3b^2 - 1}\right) = \frac{3b^3 - b - b^3 + b}{3b^2 - 1} = \frac{2b^3}{3b^2 - 1}$$

□

> (Part iii) If $a = -10^6$, what is the approximate value of b?

Solution. As a becomes smaller and smaller, the slope of the line $y = m(x - a)$ gets smaller as well. When a becomes a large negative number the line will be almost horizontal.

That means, the point B where the line is tangent to the cubic will be very close to the local maxima, where the derivative is 0, and the tangent line is horizontal. So a good approximation for b is achieved by solving for the turning point between -1 and 0.

Solving the equation $f'(x) = 0 \implies 3x^2 - 1 = 0 \implies x = \pm\frac{1}{\sqrt{3}}$. Plugging in these values to $f''(x) = 6x$, we see that the local maximum is at

$$x = -1/\sqrt{3}$$

□

(Part iv) Using the fact that $x^3 - x - m(x - a) = (x - b)^2(x - c)$ (which you need not prove), show that $c = -2b$.

Solution. If we expand $(x - b)^2(x - c)$ and compare the coefficients of x^2 we get $0 = -2b - c$ and so $c = -2b$. □

(Part v) R is the finite region bounded above by the line $y = m(x - a)$ and bounded below by the cubic $y = x^3 - x$. For what value of a is the area of R largest?

Show that the largest possible area of R is $\frac{27}{4}$.

Solution. We can see that as a increases and gets closer to -1, the tangent line rises and the area of R increases. Hence, the largest area should be when $a = -1$.

If $a = -1$, then b is also -1, and the line $y = m(x - a)$ is the tangent to the cubic at -1. We also have, $c = 2$ by Part iv.

If $a = -1$, the equation of the line is $y = 2x + 2$, which intersects the graph again at $(2, 6)$.

Hence the largest area achieved by R is

$$\int_{-1}^{2} [2(x+1) - (x^3 - x)] \, dx = \int_{-1}^{2} [3x + 2 - x^3] \, dx = \left[\frac{3x^2}{2} + 2x - \frac{x^4}{4}\right]_{-1}^{2}$$

$$= (6 + 4 - 4) - \left(\frac{3}{2} - 2 - \frac{1}{4}\right) = \frac{27}{4}$$

□

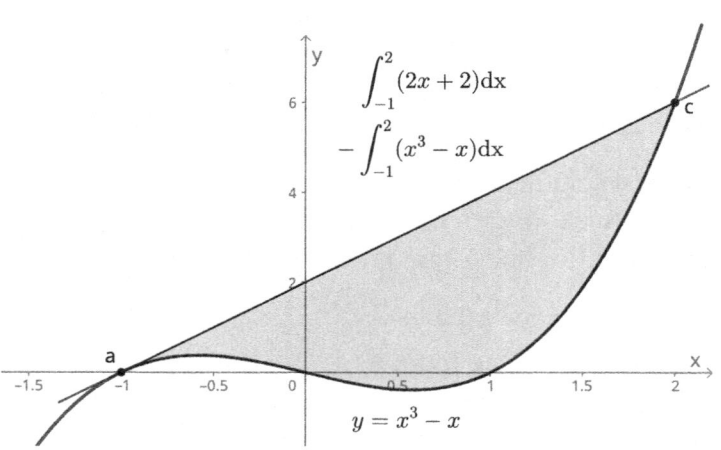

Figure 8.5

CHAPTER 9
Graph Transformation

9.1 Plotting common functions

In the MAT, you will be often asked to draw a rough sketch of a given function, or to identify the graph of a function in the MCQ section. To tackle these questions, you need a strong understanding of the various properties of a function that define the shape of the function once plotted on a graph. We will first see some functions you need to be comfortable plotting, and then explore ways you can figure out the shape of a function you haven't seen before.

Trigonometric functions

We start with the basic trigonometric functions: $\sin, \cos, \tan$.

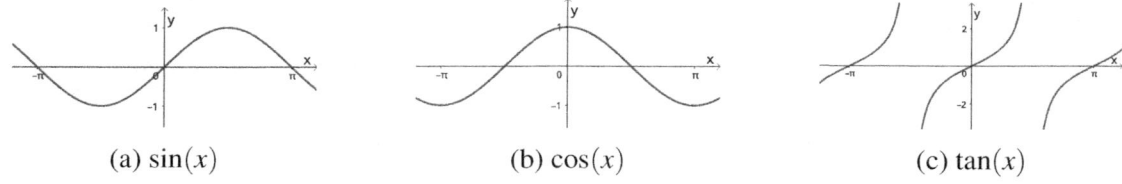

(a) $\sin(x)$ (b) $\cos(x)$ (c) $\tan(x)$

Figure 9.1: Trigonometric functions

Things to notice in these graphs:

1. sin and cos lie between $-1, 1$, are periodic with period 2π

2. $\sin 0 = 0, \cos 0 = 1$, sin is a translation of cos in positive x direction by $\frac{\pi}{2}$.

3. $\tan 0 = 0$, tan takes value in all of $\mathbb{R}$, and $\tan x \to \infty$ as $x \to \pi$ or $x \to -\pi$

4. The roots of $\sin x$ are $n\pi$, and the roots of $\cos x$ are $(2n+1)\frac{\pi}{2}$ where n is an integer.

5. $\sin x$ achieves the maximum value at $(4n+1)\frac{\pi}{2}$ where n is an integer, and $\cos x$ achieves the maximum at $2n\pi$ where n is an integer.

6. $\sin x$ achieves the minimum at $(4n-1)\frac{\pi}{2}$ where n is an integer, and $\cos x$ achieves the maximum at $(2n+1)\pi$ where n is an integer.

Modified trigonometric functions

The unique shapes of the trigonometric functions also influence more complicated functions defined by the trigonometric functions. Below are the shapes of $\frac{\sin x}{x}, \sin^2 x$

9.1. PLOTTING COMMON FUNCTIONS

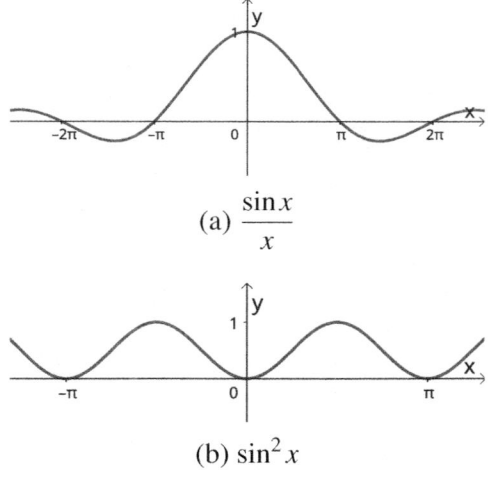

(a) $\dfrac{\sin x}{x}$

(b) $\sin^2 x$

Figure 9.2

Things to notice:

1. $\dfrac{\sin x}{x} \to 1$ as $x \to 0$, it grows smaller as x increases, but changes sign like $\sin x$ does. It has the same roots as $\sin x$, but the local maximums and minimums are different than $\sin x$. The turning points are at x where x satisfies $x = \tan x$.

2. $\sin^2 x$ lies between $0, 1$, has period π. Also, it's a horizontal translation of $\cos^2 x$ by $\frac{\pi}{2}$.

Example 9.1. MAT 2010 Question 1.D Which of the graphs below is a sketch of
$$y = \sin^2 \sqrt{x}$$

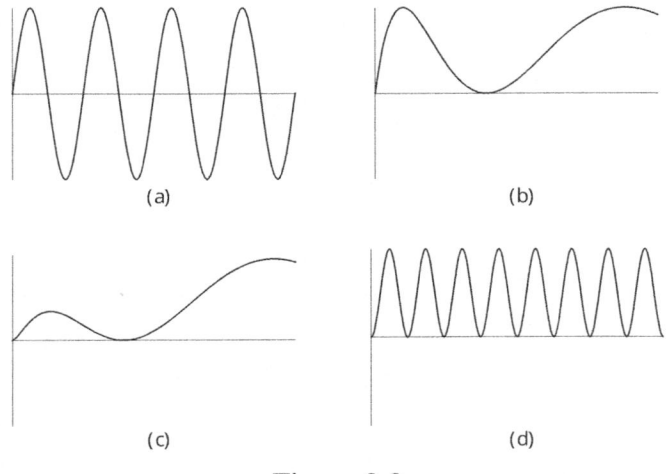

Figure 9.3

Solution. The given function is $y = \sin^2 \sqrt{x}$.

y can only take positive values, so we can discard a as an option.

Between two roots of $\sin^2 \sqrt{x}$, the maximum value of y is 1, so we can discard c.

The solutions to $\sin \sqrt{x} = 0$ are of the form $(n\pi)^2$, so b is the solution. □

Quadratic functions

A quadratic function of the form $y = ax^2 + bx + c$ can have $2, 1, 0$ roots. Below are graphs of quadratic functions with $a > 0$.

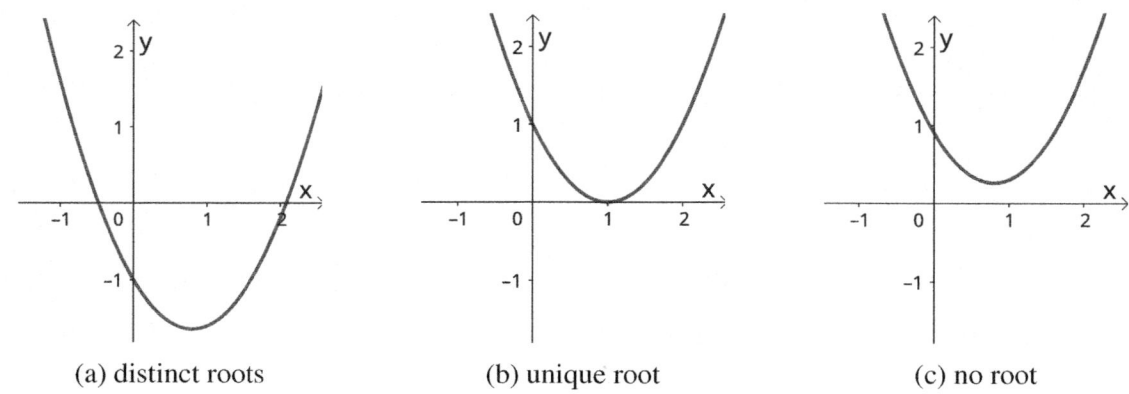

(a) distinct roots (b) unique root (c) no root

Things to notice:

1. If $a > 0$, then the function has a global minimum.

9.1. PLOTTING COMMON FUNCTIONS

2. If $a < 0$, then it will be upside down, and will have a global maximum instead.

3. If $b^2 - 4ac > 0$, then y has two roots, and the plot of y intersects the x axis twice.

4. If $b^2 - 4ac = 0$, then it has one root, and the plot touches the x axis.

5. Otherwise it has no root, and the plot does not intersect the x axis.

Cubic Function

Functions of the form $y = ax^3 + bx^2 + cx + d$ are called cubic functions.

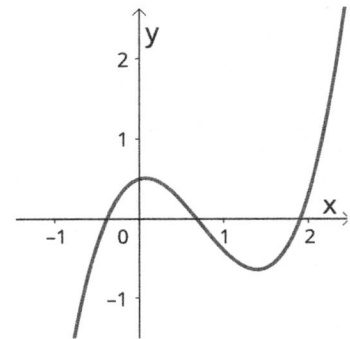

(a) three roots, two turning points

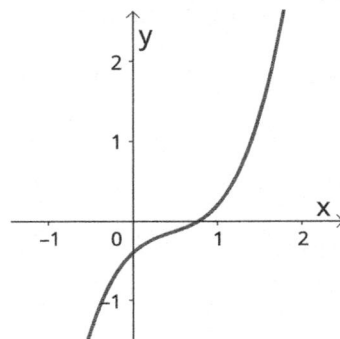

(b) one root, no turning point

Things to notice:

1. If the coefficient a of x^3 is positive, then the $y \to \infty$ as $x \to \infty$, and $y \to -\infty$ as $x \to -\infty$. If a is negative, then $y \to -\infty$ as $x \to \infty$ and $y \to \infty$ as $x \to -\infty$.

2. A cubic function always has at least one real root. So it can have either one or three real roots.

3. A cubic function can have 0, 1 or 2 turning points. If it has two turning points, one of them will be a local maximum, and the other will be a local minimum. If it has one turning point, it will be an inflection point.

Quartic Function

Polynomial functions with degree 4 are called quartic functions.

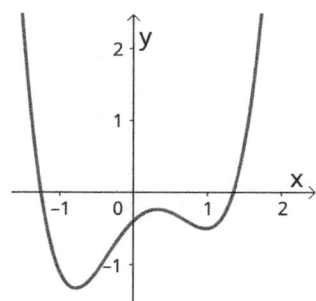
(a) 2 roots, 3 turning points

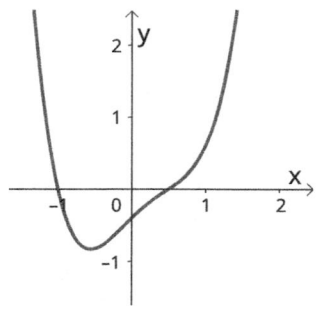
(b) 2 roots, 1 turning point

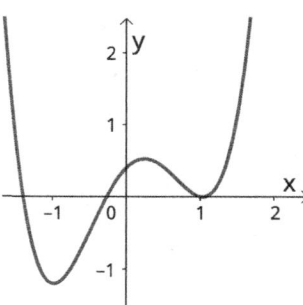
(c) 3 roots, 3 turning points

Things to notice:

1. A quartic function can have $0, 2$ or 4 roots.

2. It can have 1 or 3 turning points because the first derivative will be a cubic polynomial.

3. In the third graph, 2 is a double root, because it's also a root of the first derivative.

Example 9.2 (MAT 2011 Question 1.A). A sketch of the graph $y = x^3 - x^2 - x + 1$ appears on which of the following?

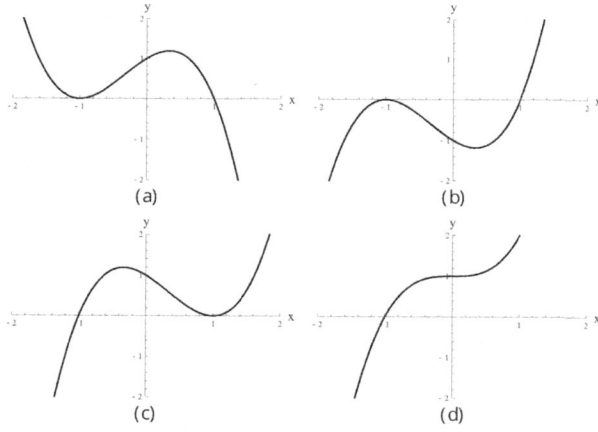

Figure 9.7

Solution. The given function is
$$f(x) = x^3 - x^2 - x + 1 = (x^2 - 1)(x - 1) = (x - 1)^2(x + 1)$$
so it has two distinct roots at $-1, 1$, and 1 is a double root.

The only option that shows 1 as a double root is (c). □

9.2. RELATION BETWEEN $F(X)$ AND $F'(X)$

Example 9.3 (MAT 2012 Question 1.2). Which one of the following equations could possibly have the graph given below?

1. $y = (3-x)^2(3+x)^2(1-x)$
2. $y = -x^2(x-9)\left(x^2-3\right)$
3. $y = (x-6)(x-2)^2(x+2)^2$
4. $y = \left(x^2-1\right)^2(3-x)$

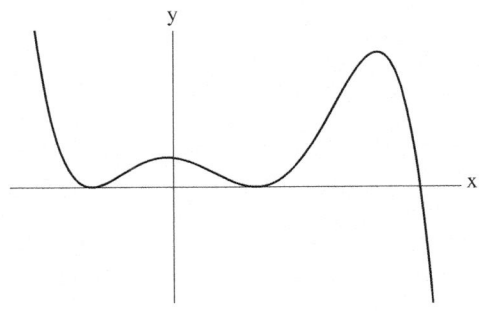

Figure 9.8

Solution. All the functions are quintic functions, so the graph has to be quintic as well.

0 is not a root, so that eliminates 2.

As the function is quintic, and it's values at negative x are positive, the leading coefficient must be negative. So that eliminates 3.

The graph has three distinct roots, two of which are positive. Furthermore, the smaller positive root is a double root. But in 1, the greater positive root is a double root.

So the function is 4. □

9.2 Relation between $f(x)$ and $f'(x)$

$f'(x)$ as rate of change

We know $f'(x)$ at a point represents the rate at which $f(x)$ changes at that point. For example

1. At A_1, f decreases rather rapidly, so $f'(a)$ is a smaller negative number.
2. At B_1 f increases, so $f'(b)$ is positive.
3. C_1 is a turning point, so $f'(c) = 0$.
4. At D_1 f increases very fast, so $f'(d)$ is a bigger positive number.

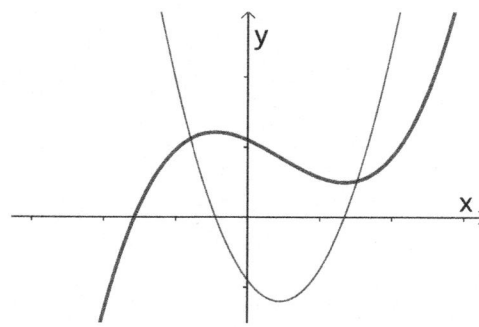

Figure 9.9: $f(x)$ in the cubic and $f'(x)$ is the quadratic

Convexity with f''

$f''(x)$ has two roots, at $M = (m,0)$ and $N = (n,0)$.

1. $f''(x) > 0$ on $(-\infty, m)$, so f' is increasing and f is convex on $(-\infty, m)$.
2. $f''(x) \leq 0$ on $[m,n]$, so f' is decreasing and f is concave on $[m,n]$.
3. $f''(x) > 0$ on (n, ∞), so f' is increasing and f is convex on (n, ∞).

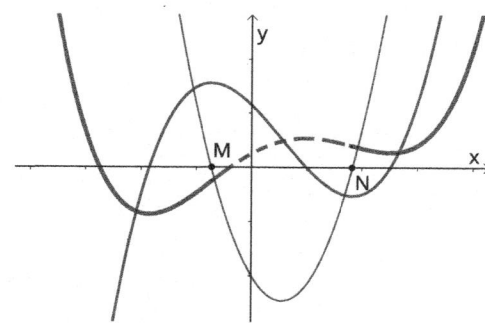

Figure 9.10: $f(x)$ is the quadric, $f'(x)$ is the cubic and $f''(x)$ is the quadratic function

9.2. RELATION BETWEEN $F(X)$ AND $F'(X)$

Example 9.4 (MAT 2020 Question 1.H). The following five graphs are, in some order, plots of $y = f(x), y = g(x), y = h(x), y = \frac{df}{dx}$ and $y = \frac{dg}{dx}$; that is, three unknown functions and the derivatives of the first two of those functions. Which graph is a plot of $h(x)$?

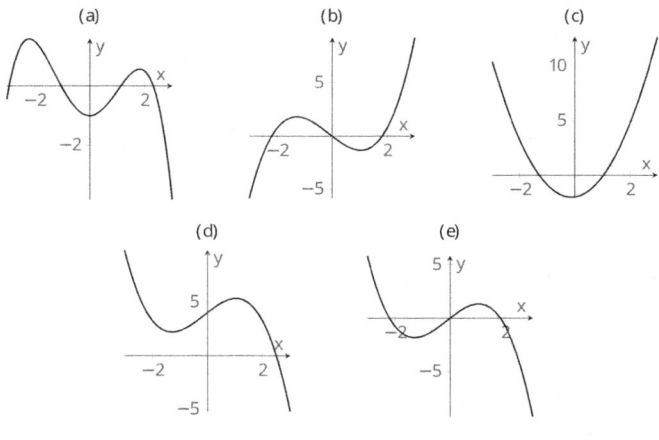

Figure 9.11

Solution. There are three cubic functions, so if (a) (a quartic function) is not either f or g, then there should've been at least two quadratic functions. So the quintic function has to be either f or g. Say it's f.

Notice that f (a) has three turning points, so is increasing at very negative. (b) and (e) both have three real roots, but (e) is positive at very negative, so (e) is the derivative of f.

(c) has to be g'. Now, g' is positive at negative, so g needs to be increasing at negative. So (b) has to be g.

This leaves option (d) for h. □

Recognising graphs

As demonstrated in previous examples, you can recognise the connection between a function and its graph by

1. Looking at the roots.

2. Looking at the turning points.

3. Finding out intervals where the function is increasing/decreasing or convex/concave and relating that information with f' and f''.

4. Occasionally you might plug in some values into the equation to see if the graph passes through those points.

Example 9.5 (MAT 2013 Question 1.D). Which of the graphs below is a sketch of
$$x^4 - y^2 = 2y + 1$$

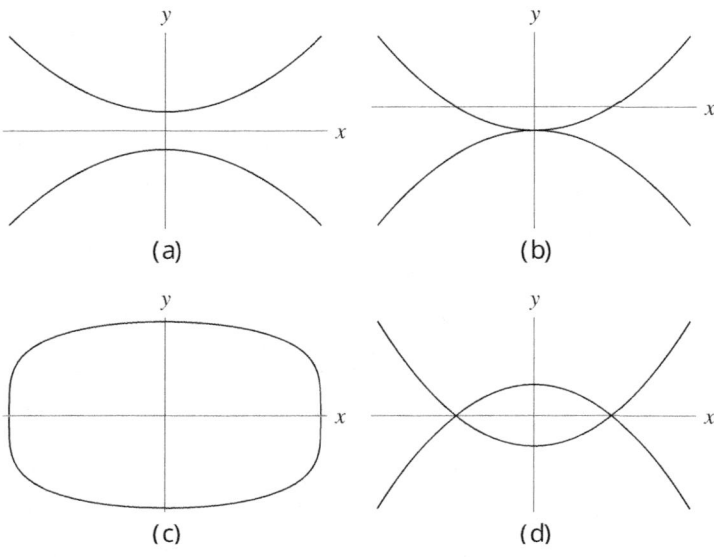

Figure 9.12

Solution. Plugging in value of $x = 0$ into the equation, we see that $y^2 + 2y + 1 = 0$, so $(0, -1)$ is the only place the graph will intersect the y-axis.

Since (b) is the only graph that has this property, (b) is the sketch of the equation. □

Example 9.6 (MAT 2008 Question 1.G). Which of the graphs below is a sketch of
$$y = \frac{1}{4x - x^2 - 5}$$

9.3. TRANSFORMATIONS

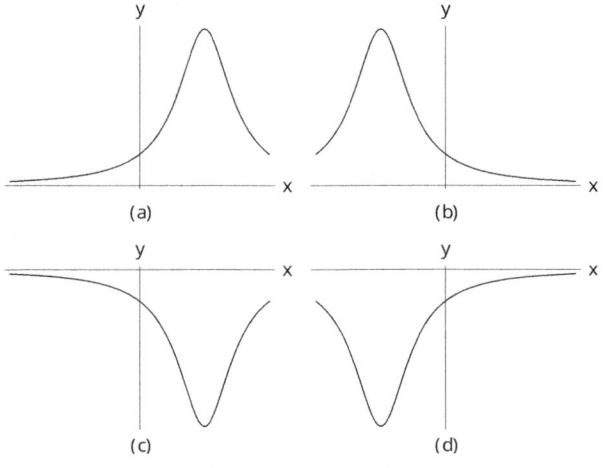

Figure 9.13

Solution. Let $f(x) = -x^2 + 4x - 5$, then $y = \frac{1}{f(x)}$. Since $f(x)$ has leading coefficient negative, it attains negative value for larger value of x. So y also has negative values. This eliminates (a) and (b).

Now, $f'(x) = -2x + 4$, so f has the maximum value at 2, and y has its minimum at 2.

Hence we have our solution (c). □

9.3 Transformations

Translation

Moving a curve without deforming it is called **Translation**. If f is a curve on the plane, then we have the following translations

1. Vertical translation: moving the curve in the y direction. This has the form $f(x) + c$, where $c > 0$ corresponds to a shift upwards and $c < 0$ downwards.

2. Horizontal translation: moving the curve in the x direction. This has the form $f(x+c)$, where $c > 0$ corresponds to a shift to the left and $c < 0$ to the right.

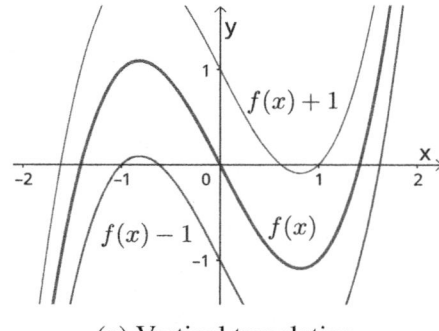

(a) Vertical translation

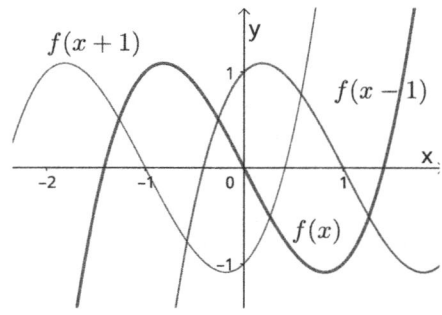

(b) Horizontal translation

Dilation

Shrinking or expanding a curve without moving it is called **Dilation**. If f is a curve on the plane, the we have the following dilations

1. **Vertical dilation**: stretching the curve in the y direction. This has the form $cf(x)$, where $c > 1$ corresponds to a stretch and $c < 1$ to a shrink.

2. **Horizontal dilation**: stretching the curve in the x direction. This has the form $f(cx)$, where $c < 1$ corresponds to a stretch and negative $c > 1$ to a shrink.

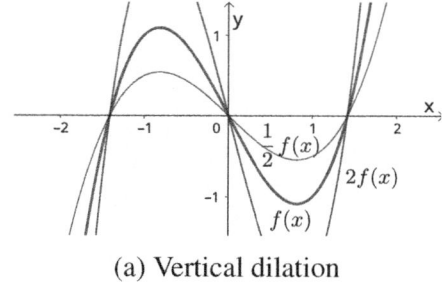

(a) Vertical dilation

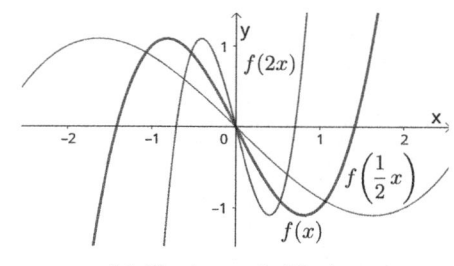

(b) Horizontal dilation

Reflection

Reflection is a transformation that flips the curve with respect to a mirror line. If f is a curve on the plane, then we have the following reflections

1. **Vertical reflection**: reflecting with respect to the x-axis. This has the form $-f(x)$.

2. **Horizontal reflection**: reflecting with respect to the y-axis. This has the form $f(-x)$.

9.3. TRANSFORMATIONS

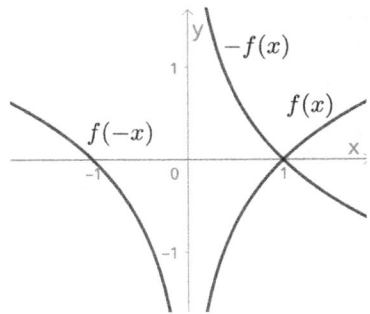

Figure 9.16

Examples

Example 9.7 (MAT Specimen b Question 1.B). The diagram below shows the graph of the function $y = f(x)$. The graph of the function $y = -f(x+1)$ is drawn in which of the following diagrams?

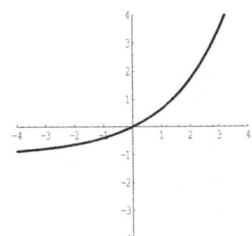

Figure 9.17

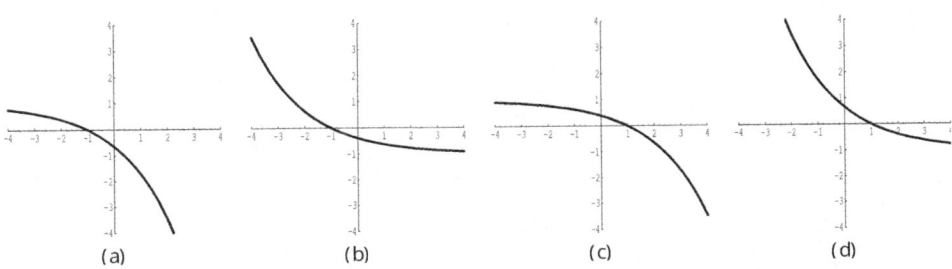

Figure 9.18

Solution. First, we translate the curve to turn it into $f(x+1)$, then we reflect it with respect to the x axis to get $-f(x+1)$ □

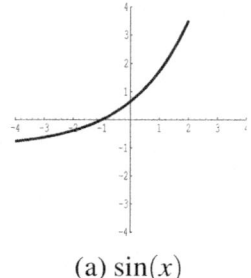
(a) sin(x)

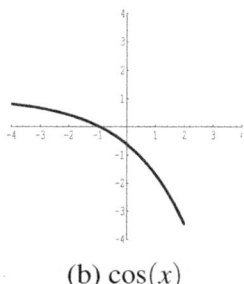
(b) cos(x)

Example 9.8 (MAT 2013 Question 1.B). The graph of $y = \sin x$ is reflected first in the line $x = \pi$ and then in the line $y = 2$. What is the equation of the resulting graph?

Solution. Drawing a graph is helpful in this problem. First, notice that after reflecting in the line $x = \pi$, the bump between $0, \pi$ will become a bump between $\pi, 2\pi$, so it's akin to translating the graph by π to the right.

So the graph will be $\sin(x - \pi) = -\sin x$.

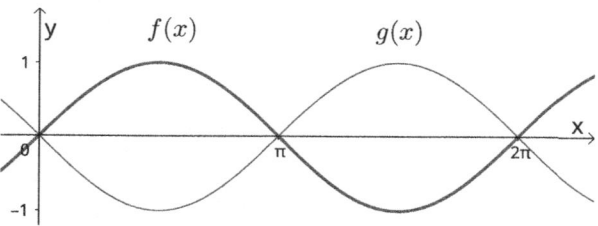

Figure 9.20

Now, if we reflect $-\sin x$ on $y = 2$, the bumps will be reverted, so it will just be translating $\sin x$ upwards by a constant.

Calculating the value at 0, we see that the resulting graph must be $\sin x + 4$

9.3. TRANSFORMATIONS

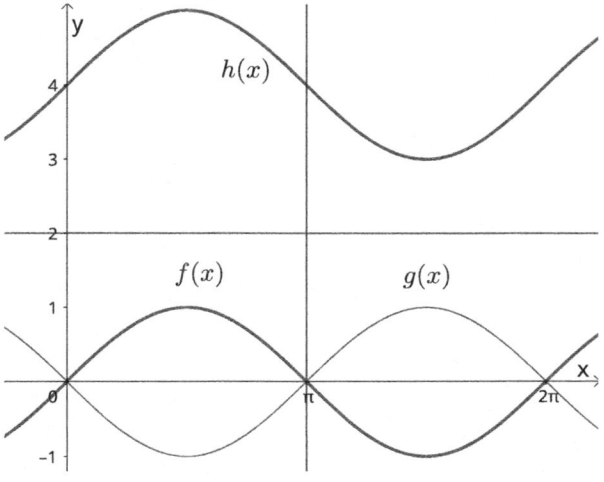

Figure 9.21

Example 9.9. Given a curve $f(x)$, sketch $-2f(2x+1)+2$?

Solution. 1. First, we sketch the horizontal dilation $f(2x)$

2. Then the translation $f(2x+1)$

3. Then the vertical dilation $2f(2x+1)$

4. Then the vertical reflection $-2f(2x+1)$

5. Then the vertical translation $-2f(2x+1)+2$

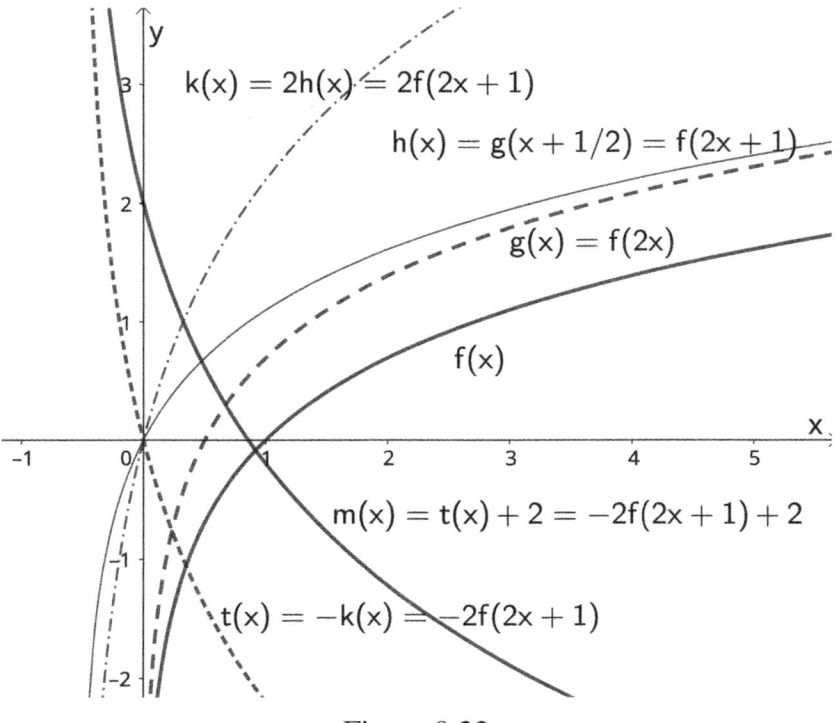

Figure 9.22

Tips

1. Be careful with the interpretation of $f(x)+1$ or $f(x)-1$, and $f(ax)$ where $a<1$ or not.

2. For complicated transformations as shown in the last example, do each transformation individually.

3. Often, simply plugging in sample values will help determine the shape.

CHAPTER 10
Sequences and Series

10.1 Arithmetic and Geometric Series

Arithmetic Sequence

An arithmetic sequence is where there is a common difference between any two consecutive terms. If the starting value is a and the common difference is d, then the terms of the sequence are:
$$a, a+d, a+2d, \ldots$$

And the nth term of the sequence has the form $a + (n-1)d$.

Arithmetic Series

A series is a sum of some terms. Like $a+b+c+d\ldots$. An arithmetic series is a series where the terms form an arithmetic sequence.

We denote the sum of the first n terms of an arithmetic series by S_n. To find a closed form or S_n, we use the Gaussian trick of writing S_n backwards, and considering $S_n + S_n$:

$$
\begin{array}{llllll}
S_n = a & + (a+d) & + \ldots + (a+(n-1)d) & + (a+(n-1)d) \\
S_n = (a+(n-1)d) & + (a+(n-2)d) & + \ldots + (a+d) & + a \\
\hline
2S_n = (2a+nd) & + (2a+nd) & + \ldots + (2a+nd) & + (2a+nd)
\end{array}
$$

Giving us the formula:

$$S_n = \sum_{k=1}^{n} a + (k-1)d = \frac{n}{2}(2a + (n-1)d) = na + d\frac{n(n-1)}{2}$$

Geometric Sequences

A geometric sequence is where there is a common ratio between any two consecutive terms. If the starting value is a and the common ratio is r, then the terms of the sequence are–

$$a, ar, ar^2, ar^3 \ldots$$

And the nth term of the sequence has the form ar^{n-1}.

Geometric Series

A geometric series is where the terms make an geometric sequence. If we denote the sum of the first n terms of a geometric series is given by S_n, then S_n has the form:

$$S_n = \sum_{k=1}^{n} ar^{k-1} = a\frac{r^n - 1}{r - 1}$$

How do we get this closed form? We use a similar technique as before:

$$
\begin{aligned}
rS_n = &\quad\quad ar \quad + \ldots + ar^{n-2} + ar^{n-r} + ar^n \\
S_n = &\; a + ar \quad + \ldots + ar^{n-2} + ar^{n-r} \\
\hline
rS_n - S_n = &\quad ar^n - a
\end{aligned}
$$

Sum of infinite geometric series

An infinite series is one where there are infinitely many terms. Note that, if a geometric series has a common ratio of greater or equal than 1, then the sum of the series will be infinitely large, and we can't calculate it.

However, if the common ratio is less than one, that is, $|r| < 1$, the sum of the infinite series

$$a + ar + ar^2 + ar^3 + \ldots$$

converges to

$$a + ar + ar^2 + ar^3 + \cdots = \frac{a}{1-r}$$

What does "converges" mean here?

Since we can't possibly calculate the sum of an infinite series, we instead "approximate" the infinite sum by a finite sum: S_n, by taking the first n terms of the series.

Now, we know $S_n = a\frac{r^n - 1}{r - 1}$. As $|r| < 1$, for large values of n, r^n will become very small. Intuitively, we can consider r^n to be almost 0, so we can remove it from the expression, giving us the approximation $\frac{a}{1-r}$ for the sum of the infinite series.

Examples

For example,

- $1+2+\cdots+2^n = 2^{n+1}-1$

- $1+3+\cdots+3^n = \dfrac{1}{2}\left(3^{n+1}-1\right)$

- $1+\dfrac{1}{2}+\dfrac{1}{4}+\dfrac{1}{8} = \dfrac{1}{1-\frac{1}{2}} = 2$

- $1+\dfrac{1}{3}+\dfrac{1}{9}+\dfrac{1}{27}+\cdots = \dfrac{3}{4}$

But the sum does not converge when $r > 1$. For example

$$1+2+2^2+2^3+\cdots$$

grows very large very quickly. How do we know that? The sum of the first n terms of this geometric series has the form $2^{n+1}-1$, which for large values of n becomes very large, and it keeps growing to infinity.

> **Example 10.1.** Find the sum of the first $2n$ terms of
>
> $$1,\ 1,\ 2,\ \dfrac{1}{2},\ 4,\ \dfrac{1}{4},\ 8,\ \dfrac{1}{8},\ 16,\ \dfrac{1}{16}\cdots$$

Solution. Notice that this series is the combination of two well-known series:

$$1,\ 1,\ 2,\ \dfrac{1}{2},\ 4,\ \dfrac{1}{4},\ 8,\ \dfrac{1}{8},\ 16,\ \dfrac{1}{16}\cdots$$

So the first $2n$ terms will contain n terms from the sequence $1,2,4,\ldots$ and n terms from $1,\frac{1}{2},\frac{1}{4},\ldots$. We have,

$$S_{2n} = (1+2+4\cdots+2^{n-1}) + \left(1+\dfrac{1}{2}+\dfrac{1}{4}+\cdots+\dfrac{1}{2^{n-1}}\right)$$

$$= 2^n - 1 + 2 - \dfrac{1}{2^{n-1}} = 2^n + 1 - 2^{1-n}$$

So the sum is $2^n + 1 - 2^{1-n}$. □

Some special series

1. **Harmonic series**: The series $1+\frac{1}{2}+\frac{1}{3}+\cdots+\frac{1}{n}$ is called the harmonic series. As n grows to infinity, this sum of this series grows to infinity as well.

2. The series $1+\frac{1}{2^2}+\frac{1}{3^2}+\cdots+\frac{1}{n^2}$ converges as n goes to ∞, and it approaches

$$\sum_{i=1}^{\infty} \dfrac{1}{i^2} = \dfrac{\pi^2}{6}$$

10.2. RECURSIVE SEQUENCES

3. **Alternating Harmonic Series**: The series $1 - \frac{1}{2} + \frac{1}{3} - \frac{1}{4} \ldots$ converges, and is equal to $\sum_{i=1}^{\infty}(-1)^{i-1}\frac{1}{i} = \ln(2)$.

10.2 Recursive sequences

An infinite sequence whose terms depend on the terms in the sequence before it is called a recursive sequence.

Probably the most famous recursive sequence is the Fibonacci sequence F_n, which is defined by
$$F_0 = 0, F_1 = 1, F_n = F_{n-1} + F_{n-2}$$
The first few terms of this sequence are:
$$0, 1, 1, 2, 3, 5, 8, 13, 21, 34, 55 \ldots$$

Solving recursive sequences

Solving a recursive sequence refers to finding a closed form of the terms of the sequences, that doesn't depend on the previous terms.

Suppose for example we have a recursive sequence defined by $a_0 = 1$, $a_n = 2a_{n-1} + 1$.

Listing the first few terms, we get
$$a_0 = 1, a_1 = 3, a_2 = 7, a_3 = 15, \ldots$$

Which suggests that the $a_n = 2^{n+1} - 1$, which we can easily prove by induction. Here, the form of a_n only depends on the value n, not on any other a_i.

> **Example 10.2** (MAT 2011 Question 1.I). The function $f(n)$ is defined for positive integers n according to the rules
> $$f(1) = 1, \quad f(2n) = f(n), \quad f(2n+1) = (f(n))^2 - 2$$
> What is the value of $f(1) + f(2) + f(3) + \cdots + f(100)$?

Solution. The first step to solving any recursive sequence problem is to calculate the first few terms and look for patterns.

Here the first few terms are:

$$f(1) = 1, f(2) = f(1) = 1, f(3) = f(1)^2 - 2 = -1, f(4) = 1$$

$$f(5) = f(2)^2 - 2 = -1, f(6) = -1, f(7) = f(3)^2 - 2 = -1, f(8) = 1$$

By looking at the leading terms we get the hunch that $f(n) = \pm 1$ for all n.

How do we prove this? First note that for all i, n, $f(2^i n) = f(n)$.

Now if we inductively assume that for all $k < n$, $f(k) = \pm 1$, then we have

$$f(n) = \begin{cases} -1 & \text{if } n \text{ is odd} \\ f(\frac{n}{2}) & \text{otherwise, which is also } \pm 1 \end{cases}$$

So we've proved $f(n) = \pm 1$. How do we know whether its 1 or -1?

If n is odd, then surely $f(n) = -1$. And we know $f(2^i n) = f(n) = -1$ for all i.

So $f(n) = 1$ only if $f(n) = 2^i \times 1$ for some i. Hence we reach the conclusion,

$$f(n) = \begin{cases} 1 & \text{if } n = 2^i \text{ for some } i \\ -1 & \text{otherwise} \end{cases}$$

Now as there are only 7 powers of 2 less than 100: $1, 2, 4, 8, 16, 31, 64$, we have:

$$f(1) + f(2) + \cdots + f(100) = 1 \times 7 + (-1) \times 93 = -86$$

□

Tips on solving recursive sequences

1. Always begin by calculating some leading terms of the sequence.

2. Try to notice patterns. If you have a hypothesis, try proving it using induction.

3. In the MAT exam, you won't be asked to solve complicated recursive sequences, so look for simple patterns.

4. Often, the sequences will turn out to be either arithmetic, geometric, or periodic. These are the most common kind of sequences you'll encounter on the MAT, so keep an eye out for them.

Common traps

1. Be careful when writing down recursions. Think about all the cases carefully.

2. Sometimes the question might ask you to prove a property of a recursion. Don't be tricked into thinking you MUST find a closed form for the term.

10.3 Walkthrough: MAT 2016 Question 5

Question

This question concerns the sum s_n defined by

$$s_n = 2 + 8 + 24 + \cdots + n2^n$$

Part i Let $f(n) = (An+B)2^n + C$ for constants A, B and C yet to be determined, and suppose $s_n = f(n)$ for all $n \geqslant 1$.

By setting $n = 1, 2, 3$, find three equations that must be satisfied by A, B and C.

Part ii Solve the equations from part (i) to obtain values for A, B and C.

Part iii Using these values, show that if $s_k = f(k)$ for some $k \geqslant 1$ then $s_{k+1} = f(k+1)$.

You may now assume $s_n = f(n)$ for all $n \geq 1$.

Part iv Find simplified expressions for the following sums:

$$t_n = n + 2(n-1) + 4(n-2) + 8(n-3) + \cdots + 2^{n-1}1$$
$$u_n = \frac{1}{2} + \frac{2}{4} + \frac{3}{8} + \cdots + \frac{n}{2^n}$$

Part v Find the sum $\sum_{k=1}^{n} s_k$

Solution

> (Part i) Let $f(n) = (An+B)2^n + C$ for constants A, B and C yet to be determined, and suppose $s_n = f(n)$ for all $n \geq 1$.
>
> By setting $n = 1, 2, 3$, find three equations that must be satisfied by A, B and C.

Solution. It's as straightforward as plugging in the values of n in three different equations:

$$s_1 = 2(A+B) + C = 2, \quad s_2 = 4(2A+B) + C = 10, \quad s_3 = 8(3A+B) + C = 34$$

> (Part ii) Solve the equations from part (i) to obtain values for A, B and C.

Solution. The three equations form a system of equations with three variables, so we can find solutions using basic techniques.

Subtracting the first equation from the other two gives

$$6A + 2B = 8$$
$$22A + 6B = 32,$$

hence $4A = 8$, so $A = 2, B = -2, C = 2$.

> (Part iii) Using these values, show that if $s_k = f(k)$ for some $k \geq 1$ then $s_{k+1} = f(k+1)$.

Solution. Notice that this is the inductive step in a proof by induction. For the values of A, B, C we calculated previously, we want to validate our assumption that $s_k = f(k)$ for all natural number k.

Suppose for some $k \geq 1$, $s_k = f(k) = (2k-2)2^k + 2$. We have,

$$\begin{aligned} s_{k+1} &= f(k) + (k+1)2^{k+1} \\ &= (k-1)2^{k+1} + 2 + (k+1)2^{k+1} \\ &= k2^{k+2} + 2 = f(k+1) \end{aligned}$$

as required.

10.3. WALKTHROUGH: MAT 2016 QUESTION 5

Alternatively, we can write s_n as

$$s_n = 1 \times 2 + 2 \times 4 + 3 \times 8 + \ldots n \times 2^n$$
$$= (2 + 4 + 8 + \cdots + 2^n) + (4 + 8 + \cdots + 2^n) + (8 + \cdots + 2^n) \cdots + (2^n)$$
$$= 2^{n+2} - 2 + \cdots + 2^{n+1} - 2^n$$
$$= n2^{n+1} - (2^{n+1} - 2)$$

Putting these together with the initial values of s_1, s_2, s_3, we have shown that $s_n = (2n-2)2^n + 2$. □

> You may now assume $s_n = f(n)$ for all $n \geq 1$.
>
> (Part iv) Find simplified expressions for the following sums:
>
> $$t_n = n + 2(n-1) + 4(n-2) + 8(n-3) + \cdots + 2^{n-1}1$$
> $$u_n = \frac{1}{2} + \frac{2}{4} + \frac{3}{8} + \cdots + \frac{n}{2^n}$$

Solution. We have

$$t_n = (n + 2n + 4n + \cdots + 2^n \cdot n) - (2 + 8 + 24 + \ldots + 2^n \cdot n)$$
$$= n(2^{n+1} - 1) - f(n) = n(2^{n+1} - 1) - (n-1)2^{n+1} - 2$$
$$= 2^{n+1} - n - 2$$

Now $u_n = \dfrac{t_n}{2^n}$, so $u_n = 2 - \dfrac{n+2}{2^n}$ □

> (Part v) Find the sum $\displaystyle\sum_{k=1}^{n} s_k$

Solution. We manipulate the summation sign:

$$\sum_{k=1}^{n} s_k = \sum_{k=1}^{n} \left(2k2^k - 2^{k+1} + 2\right)$$
$$= \sum_{k=1}^{n} \left(k2^{k+1}\right) - \sum_{k=1}^{n} \left(2^{k+1}\right) + \sum_{k=1}^{n} 2$$
$$= 2\sum_{k=1}^{n} \left(k2^k\right) - 2^{n+2} + 4 + 2n$$
$$= 2f(n) - 2^{n+2} + 4 + 2n = 2^{n+2}n - 2^{n+3} + 2n + 8$$

□

CHAPTER 11

Algorithms and Games

11.1 Procedures

We will now look at some questions that deal with procedures to accomplish some result or to solve some problem.

Consider the problem of finding the binary representation of a number n. We proceed in the following ways:

1. Divide n by 2 and write down the remainder.

2. Take the quotient, divide it by 2, write down the remainder to the left of the previous number

3. Proceed by taking the next quotient.

This procedure gives us a binary representation of a given number n. In this section, we will try to find such procedures to solve particular problems.

Analysing procedures

Consider our previous example. If n is the given number, and if n can be written as: $n = 2^k + c_{k-1}2^{k-1} + \cdots + 2c_1 + c_0$, where $c_i = 0$ or 1, then we are looking for the binary representation $(1c_{k-1}c_{k-2}\ldots c_1 c_0)_2$.

How do we show that the procedure we came up with actually finds this binary representation?

Solution. We closely examine what happens at each step

1. At the first step, we divide n by 2, and write down the remainder, c_0. The quotient now is $m = 2^{k-1} + c_{k-1}2^{k-2} + \cdots + 2c_2 + c_1$

2. Then we divide m by 2, and write down the remainder, c_1 to the left of c_0.

3. So at any given point, we will have the quotient $2^{k-t} + c_{k-1}2^{k-t-1} + \cdots + 2c_{t+2} + c_{t+1}$, and the cumulative binary representation $c_t c_{t-1} \ldots c_1 c_0$.

4. On the next step, the quotient will become $2^{k-t-1} + c_{k-1}2^{k-t-2} + \cdots + c_{t+2}$, and our cumulative binary representation will grow by one and become $c_{t+1}c_t \ldots c_1 c_0$.

As the quotient is getting halved at each step, we know the procedure will terminate surely, because eventually it will become 0, when we will stop.

11.1. PROCEDURES

When the quotient becomes 0, the cumulative representation will become $(1c_{k-1} \ldots c_1 c_0)$, the binary representation of n.

Hence our procedure to find the binary representation of n actually yields the correct answer.

□

Proving that a procedure works

To understand a procedure, and to show that it produces the desired result, we need to

1. Understand what happens at each step of the procedure: what changes, what remains the same etc.

2. Understand the steps that cause a lot of changes to happen.

3. Understand what happpens after a number of steps.

Induction and **Invariants/Monovariants** are our most helpful friends when analysing a procedure.

Finding a Procedure

Suppose we have a question that we want to answer by finding a solution (a very meta statement, I know, but bear with me for a bit). How do we answer it? We can either find the direct solution, or show that such a solution exists, or provide a guaranteed procedure that will find the solution.

For example, consider the question–

Given a number n, find a way to represent n as a sum of Fibonacci numbers, such that no two consecutive Fibonacci numbers appear in the representation. We could answer it by directly finding a representation of n. Or, we could find a procedure, that **guarantees** finding the correct representation for any positive value of n!

There is no single best way to find such procedures, but we have several general tools that help in many situations. **Greedy algorithms** is one such tool.

Greedy Algorithm

In Greedy Algorithm, we try to find a procedure by choosing the **best** option available at every step.

Going back to our previous question, we would solve this question with greedy algorithm in the following way:

1. Call the number n. Find the largest Fibonacci number smaller than n. Call it F_k.

2. Write $n = F_k + n_1$.

3. Now find a Fibonacci representation of n_1 in the similar manner.

Example 11.1 (Abridged version of MAT 2018 Question 6). A positive rational number q is expressed in *friendly form* if it is written as a finite sum of reciprocals of distinct positive integers. Suggest a procedure by which any rational q with $0 < q < 1$ can be expressed in friendly form.

In the actual question, they guide you through the process of finding the following procedure for finding a friendly form for a given rational number q:

1. Let m be the smallest natural number such that $\frac{1}{m} \leq q$.

2. Write $q = \frac{1}{m} + q_1$.

3. Then compute the friendly form of q_1, and put it in the equation of q.

4. Then, we show that this gives us a friendly form of q.

Notice that this procedure is a greedy algorithm: at each step, we are finding the **largest reciprocal smaller than** q, which is the same as saying the smallest natural number m such that $\frac{1}{m} \leq q$.

Showing that this procedure yields the desired result requires quite a bit of work, which we will show at the end of this chapter. However, here is an example of this procedure in action. Suppose $q = \frac{5}{7}$.

1. 2 is the smallest integer such that $\frac{1}{2} \leq \frac{5}{7}$. So let $q_1 = \frac{5}{7} - \frac{1}{2} = \frac{3}{14}$.

2. 7 is the smallest integer such that $\frac{1}{7} \leq \frac{3}{14}$. So let $q_2 = \frac{3}{14} - \frac{1}{7} = \frac{1}{14}$.

3. 14 is the smallest integer such that $\frac{1}{14} \leq q_2$, and $q_2 = \frac{1}{14}$.

And so we have the friendly form, $\frac{5}{7} = \frac{1}{2} + \frac{1}{7} + \frac{1}{14}$.

11.2 Winning Games Mathematically

Winning Games

In problems involving games, finding a winning strategy means finding a way to play so that, **regardless of how the other person plays**, one player is going to win.

The key to solve this kind of problem is to find an invariant in the game and exploit it. The invariant has to be a certain state of the game. We are looking for a state with the following properties:

1. A person in that state cannot win the game.

2. If the other person played in that state, we can force him back to that state.

This kind of state is called a **losing position**. The positions that can send the other player to a losing position are called **winning positions**.

> **Example 11.2.** Suppose there is a stack of n stones. Two players, A and B, are playing a game of removing stones from the stack turn by turn. They can remove $1, 2$ or 3 stones in their turn. What are the winning and losing positions of this game?

Solution. Note that $n = 1, 2, 3$ are all winning positions. As the first player can just remove the entire stack in their first move.

So, 4 is a losing position, as no matter how the first player moves, the second player will always win.

But, $5, 6, 7$ are all winning positions, as the first player can force the second player to play with 4 stones, which is a losing position. Again, 8 is a losing position.

We hypothesise that if 4 divides n, the number of stones, then it's a losing position, and all the other positions are winning.

We prove this by induction. Obviously this is true for $n = 1, 2, 3, 4$. Suppose this holds for some $4n - 3, 4n - 2, 4n - 1, 4n$, that $4n$ is a losing position, but $4n - 3, 4n - 2, 4n - 1$ are winning positions.

If the game begins with $4n + 1, 4n + 2, 4n + 3$ stones, the first player can just remove $1, 2, 3$ stones respectively to force the second player into a losing position.

If the game beings with $4n+4$ stones, then no matter how the first player moves, the second player will move to $4n$, and it will be a losing position for the first player. Hence $4n+4$ is a losing position. □

11.3 Walkthrough: MAT 2018 Question 6

Question

> A positive rational number q is expressed in friendly form if it is written as a finite sum of reciprocals of distinct positive integers. For example, $\frac{4}{5} = \frac{1}{2} + \frac{1}{4} + \frac{1}{20}$.
>
> **Part i** Express the following numbers in friendly form: $\frac{2}{3}, \frac{2}{5}, \frac{23}{40}$.
>
> **Part ii** Let q be a rational number with $0 < q < 1$, and m be the smallest natural number such than $\frac{1}{m} \leqslant q$. Suppose $q = \frac{a}{b}$ and $q - \frac{1}{m} = \frac{c}{d}$ in their lowest terms. Show that $c < a$.
>
> **Part iii** Suggest a procedure by which any rational q with $0 < q < 1$ can be expressed in friendly form. Use the result in part (ii) to show that the procedure always works, generating distinct reciprocals and finishing within a finite time.
>
> **Part iv** Demonstrate your procedure by finding a friendly form for $\frac{4}{13}$.
>
> **Part v** Assuming that $\sum_{n=1}^{N} \frac{1}{n}$ increases without bound as N becomes large, show that every positive rational number can be expressed in friendly form.

Solution

> (Part i) Express the following numbers in friendly form: $\frac{2}{3}, \frac{2}{5}, \frac{23}{40}$.

Solution. After some messing around with numbers, we arrive at the following:

1. $\frac{2}{3} = \frac{1}{2} + \frac{1}{6} = \frac{1}{3} + \frac{1}{4} + \frac{1}{12}$

2. $\frac{2}{5} = \frac{1}{3} + \frac{1}{15} = \frac{1}{4} + \frac{1}{10} + \frac{1}{20} = \frac{1}{5} + \frac{1}{6} + \frac{1}{30}$

3. $\frac{23}{40} = \frac{1}{2} + \frac{1}{20} + \frac{1}{40}$

> (Part ii) Let q be a rational number with $0 < q < 1$, and m be the smallest natural number such than $\frac{1}{m} \leqslant q$. Suppose $q = \frac{a}{b}$ and $q - \frac{1}{m} = \frac{c}{d}$ in their lowest terms. Show that $c < a$.

Solution. If m is smallest such that $\frac{1}{m} \leq q$ then $m \geq 2$ and $\frac{1}{m-1} > \frac{a}{b}$.

So $a(m-1) < b$, and $am - b < a$, and so

$$\frac{a}{b} - \frac{1}{m} = \frac{am-b}{bm} = \frac{c}{d}$$

satisfies $c < a$. □

> (Part iii) Suggest a procedure by which any rational q with $0 < q < 1$ can be expressed in friendly form. Use the result in part (ii) to show that the procedure always works, generating distinct reciprocals and finishing within a finite time.

Solution. As discussed before, given any rational $q = \frac{a}{b}$ with $0 < q < 1$, we can chop off the largest possible reciprocal, and continue with the remainder $\frac{c}{d}$ with $0 \leq c < a$. Now we show that this procedure works.

Termination: Part ii suggests that continuing in this way yields a sequence of remainders with decreasing numerators, which must eventually terminate.

Correctness: Note that the reciprocals generated by the process must be distinct, because at each stage $\frac{1}{m} > \frac{q}{2}$, otherwise $\frac{1}{m-1} \leq \frac{1}{m/2} \leq q$. So if $\frac{1}{n}$ is generated later in the process, then

$$\frac{1}{n} \leq q - \frac{1}{m} < \frac{q}{2} < \frac{1}{m}$$

so $n > m$. □

> (Part iv) Demonstrate your procedure by finding a friendly form for $\frac{4}{13}$.

Solution. We see $\frac{1}{4} < \frac{4}{13} < \frac{1}{3}$, so we write $\frac{4}{13} = \frac{1}{4} + \frac{3}{52}$

Next, $\frac{1}{18} < \frac{3}{52} < \frac{1}{17}$, so we write $\frac{4}{13} = \frac{1}{4} + \frac{1}{18} + \frac{1}{468}$, and we have finished. □

> (Part v) Assuming that $\sum_{n=1}^{N} \frac{1}{n}$ increases without bound as N becomes large, show that every positive rational number can be expressed in friendly form.

Solution. Given any positive rational q, we can find the last partial sum of $\sum \frac{1}{n}$ that is $\leq q$. The remainder is then less than $\frac{1}{n+1}$.

Now our previous method suggests $\frac{1}{n+1}$ can be represented using reciprocals with denominators greater than those taken from the harmonic series. □

11.4 Walkthrough: MAT 2012 Question 7

Question

Amy and Brian play a game together, as follows. They take it in turns to write down a number from the set $\{0, 1, 2\}$, with Amy playing first. On each turn (except Amy's first turn), the player **must not** repeat the number just played by the previous player.

In their first version of the game, Brian wins if, after he plays, **the sum of all the numbers played so far is a multiple of 3**. Amy wins if Brian has not won within five rounds.

For example, Brian will win after the sequence

| 2,0 | 1,2 | 1,0 |

(where we draw a box around each round) because the sum of the numbers is 6. And, Amy wins after the sequence

| 2,0 | 1,2 | 1,2 | 0,2 | 1,2 |

Part i Show that if Amy starts by playing either 1 or 2, then Brian can immediately win.

Part ii Suppose, instead, Amy starts by playing 0. Show that Brian can always win within two rounds.

They now decide to change the rules so that Brian wins if, **after he plays, the sum of all the numbers played so far is one less than a multiple of 3**. Again, Amy wins if Brian has not won within five rounds. It is still the case that a player must not repeat the number just played previously.

Part iii Show that if Amy starts by playing either 0 or 2, then Brian can immediately win.

11.4. WALKTHROUGH: MAT 2012 QUESTION 7

Part iv Suppose, instead, Amy starts by playing 1. Explain why it cannot benefit Brian to play 2, assuming Amy plays with the best strategy.

Part v So suppose Amy starts by playing 1, and Brian then plays 0. How should Amy play next?

Part vi Assuming both play with the best strategies, who will win the game? Explain your answer.

Solution

(Part i) Show that if Amy starts by playing either 1 or 2, then Brian can immediately win.

Solution. If Amy plays 1, Brian plays 2 and wins. If Amy plays 2, Brian plays 1 and wins. □

(Part ii) Suppose, instead, Amy starts by playing 0. Show that Brian can always win within two rounds.

Solution. If Amy starts with 0, Brian can then play 1. Amy is now permitted to play 0 or 2.

If Amy plays 0, Brian plays 2 or, if Amy plays 2, Brian plays 0.

Either way Brian wins after two rounds. □

They now decide to change the rules so that Brian wins if, after he plays, the sum of all the numbers played so far is one less than a multiple of 3. Again, Amy wins if Brian has not won within five rounds. It is still the case that a player must not repeat the number just played previously.

(Part iii) Show that if Amy starts by playing either 0 or 2, then Brian can immediately win.

Solution. If Amy plays 0, Brian plays 2 to win. If Amy plays 2, Brian plays 0 to win. □

(Part iv) Suppose, instead, Amy starts by playing 1. Explain why it cannot benefit Brian to play 2, assuming Amy plays with the best strategy.

Solution. Brian playing 2 would effectively return the game to the starting position having used up one turn. Amy will continue by playing 1. If this leads to a win for Brian following the sequence 1, 2, 1, then w, then Brian could have won quicker by following 1 then w. □

> (Part v) So suppose Amy starts by playing 1, and Brian then plays 0. How should Amy play next?

Solution. After 1, 0 if Amy now plays 1 then Brian can win by playing 0. Hence Amy should play 2. □

> (Part vi) Assuming both play with the best strategies, who will win the game? Explain your answer.

Solution. We have shown that in the optimal game, the first three moves will be 1, 0, 2. So following from this, if Brian plays 0, then Amy can play 1 and win. If Brian plays 1, Amy can play 0 and win. So Amy will always win the game. □

CHAPTER 12

Number Theory

12.1 Divisibility

If a,b are two positive integers, and if a divides b without any remainder, then we say a **divides** b and write $a|b$.

If $a|b$, then by definition, there is an integer c, such that $b = ac$.

1. If $a|b$, and $a|c$, then $a|b \pm c$, $a|bc$

2. If $a|b, b|c$, then $a|c$

3. If $a|b$, then $a \leq b$.

4. If $a|b, b|a$, then $a = b$

Division theorem

If a,b are two integers, then the **division theorem** states:

There exists **unique** integers q,r with $0 \leq r < q$ such that

$$a = bq + r$$

It follows from the division theorem that b divides a if and only if $r = 0$.

Greatest Common Divisor and Bezout's Lemma

Given two positive integers a,b, we call d, the greatest number that divides both a and b the greatest common divisor (**gcd**) or the highest common factor (**hcf**), and write it as

$$d = \gcd(a,b) = \mathrm{hcf}(a,b)$$

The important **Bezout's lemma** states that, for all positive integers a,b, there exists integers x,y such that
$$ax + by = \gcd(a,b)$$

If the gcd of two numbers is 1, then we call them **coprime**.

Primes

A **prime** number is a positive integer that has only **two divisors, 1 and itself**. The prime numbers less than 100 are:

$$2, 3, 5, 7, 11, 13, 17, 19, 23,$$
$$29, 31, 37, 41, 43, 47, 53, 59,$$
$$61, 67, 71, 73, 79, 83, 89, 97$$

Note that, because of their definition, every two prime numbers are coprime to each other. Also, If p is a prime number and $p|ab$, then p **either divides** a **or** b.

The **Fundamental Theorem of Arithmetic** states that, every positive integer greater than 1 can be written uniquely as a product of prime numbers. For example, $660 = 2^2 \times 3 \times 5 \times 11$.

Number System and Digits

Base d representation

When we write a number, we write it in base 10. What that means is, we count the numbers using 10 digits and interpret the number 5481, for example, as $5 \times 1000 + 4 \times 100 + 8 \times 10 + 1$. For verbosity, we write $(5481)_{10}$ to indicate that we wrote the number in base 10.

Now if we want to represent the number n in any arbitrary base $d > 1$, what we are trying to find is a sequence of $k+1$ numbers, c_i, each with $0 \leq c_i < d$, and

$$n = c_k d^k + c_{k-1} d^{k-1} + \cdots + c_1 d + c_0$$

The most commonly used bases other than 10 are $2, 8, 16$, which you might recognise as binary, octal, or hexadecimal representation.

Converting a number to base d representation

Recall that we want to find c_i, such that $0 \leq c_i < d$ and

$$n = c_k d^k + c_{k-1} d^{k-1} + \cdots + c_1 d + c_0$$

We do this by repeatedly dividing n by d and listing the remainder from right to left. For example, to convert $(45)_{10}$ to base 3, we do:

$$45 = 3 \times 15 + 0 \implies c_0 = 0$$
$$15 = 3 \times 5 + 0 \implies c_1 = 0$$
$$5 = 3 \times 1 + 2 \implies c_2 = 2$$
$$1 = 3 \times 0 + 1 \implies c_3 = 1$$

So, $(45)_{10} = (1200)_3$.

12.2 Walkthrough: MAT 2015 Question 2

Question

Part i Expand and simplify

$$(a-b)\left(a^n + a^{n-1}b + a^{n-2}b^2 + \cdots + ab^{n-1} + b^n\right)$$

Part ii The prime number 3 has the property that it is one less than a square number. Are there any other prime numbers with this property? Justify your answer.

Part iii Find all the prime numbers that are one more than a cube number. Justify your answer.

Part iv Is $3^{2015} - 2^{2015}$ a prime number? Explain your reasoning carefully.

Part v Is there a positive integer k for which $k^3 + 2k^2 + 2k + 1$ is a cube number? Explain your reasoning carefully.

Solution

(Part i) Expand and simplify

$$(a-b)\left(a^n + a^{n-1}b + a^{n-2}b^2 + \cdots + ab^{n-1} + b^n\right)$$

Solution. This is simple algebra. By expanding, we get

$$a^{n+1} + a^n b + a^{n-1}b^2 + \ldots + a^2 b^{n-1} + ab^n - a^n b - a^{n-1}b^2 - \ldots - ab^n - b^{n+1}$$

12.2. WALKTHROUGH: MAT 2015 QUESTION 2

Cancelling out the terms gives $a^{n+1} - b^{n+1}$. □

> (Part ii) The prime number 3 has the property that it is one less than a square number. Are there any other prime numbers with this property? Justify your answer.

Solution. We want an integer n such that $n^2 - 1$ is a prime. But we know $n^2 - 1 = (n-1)(n+1)$. So for $n^2 - 1$ to be a prime, either of these numbers need to be 1, or else the number will have two divisors, none of which is 1. Hence it's not a prime.

As $n + 1 > 1$, we definitely need $n - 1 = 1$, that gives us the only such prime number, 3. □

> (Part iii) Find all the prime numbers that are one more than a cube number. Justify your answer.

Solution. We want an integer n such that $n^3 + 1$ is a prime number. Since we have $n^3 + 1 = (n+1)(n^2 - n + 1)$, we need either of these numbers to be 1. As $n + 1 > 1$, we must have

$$n^2 - n + 1 = 1 \implies n^2 - n = 0 \implies n = 0 \text{ or } 1$$

As $0^3 + 1 = 1$ is not a prime, the only prime of this form is $1^3 + 1 = 2$. □

> (Part iv) Is $3^{2015} - 2^{2015}$ a prime number? Explain your reasoning carefully.

Solution. Using the formula found in Part i, we have,

$$3^{2015} - 2^{2015} = \left(3^5 - 2^5\right)\left(3^{2010} + 3^{2005} \cdot 2^5 + 3^{2000} \cdot 2^{10} + \ldots + 3^5 \cdot 2^{2005} + 2^{2010}\right)$$

But neither factor is 1, so $3^{2015} - 2^{2015}$ is not prime. □

> (Part v) Is there a positive integer k for which $k^3 + 2k^2 + 2k + 1$ is a cube number? Explain your reasoning carefully.

Solution. Note that $(k)^3 < k^3 + 2k^2 + 2k$. Also note that $(k+1)^3 = k^3 + 3k^2 + 3k + 1$.

So for $k > 0$ we have

$$k^3 < k^3 + 2k^2 + 2k + 1 < (k+1)^3$$

So $k^3 + 2k^2 + 2k + 1$ lies between two consecutive cubes, hence it can't be a cube number. □

CHAPTER **13**
Combinatorics and Probability

13.1 Combinatorics

Basic counting rules

Suppose set A has a elements, B has b elements.

Addition Rule The number of ways to pick one element from A or B is $a + b$

Product Rule The number of ways to pick one element from A and B is ab

Permutations

Suppose we want to arrange the numbers $1, 2, 3 \ldots n$ in a row arbitrarily. How many ways can we do it?

We can think of choosing an arrangement as follows:

1. Choosing any of the numbers for the initial position
2. For the second position, we have $n - 1$ options left
3. For the third position, we have $n - 2$ options left
4. and so on...

Since we are picking one number for the first position, as well as another for the second place and then a third for the third place and so on, the total number of ways is given by the **Product rule**:
$$n \times (n-1) \times \cdots \times 2 \times 1 = n!$$

Over-counting

Suppose we are told to rearrange the letters *AABC*, how many ways can it be done?

It's not 4!, because then we would be counting the specific arrangement *AABC* twice!

An easy way to fix this is to divide the total number of rearrangements by 2. So we get $\frac{4!}{2} = 12$ ways of rearranging the letters.

Now suppose we are told to rearrange the letters *AAABBC*. This time two letters that have multiple instances.

13.1. COMBINATORICS

Note that if we, for now, distinguish between the $A's$ and $B's$ by giving them different names: $A_1A_2A_3B_1B_2C$, then there are 6! ways to rearrange these 6 "distinct" letters.

Now notice that, B_1, B_2 are the same, so we are counting every rearrangement **twice** with the two variations $AAAB_1B_2C$ and $AAAB_2B_1C$, so we need to divide the total by 2.

Also, we are counting every rearrangement 6 **times** with the 6 variations of $A's$:

$$A_1A_2A_3BBC, A_2A_1A_3BBC, A_1A_3A_2BBC$$

and so on. So we actually have $\frac{6!}{6 \times 2} = \frac{6!}{3! \times 2!}$ ways to rearrange the letters.

Combinations

Suppose we want to pick k items from the set $\{1, 2, \ldots n\}$. How do we do it?

We can think of this as

1. For the first item we have n options

2. $n-1$ options for the second item

3. $n-2$ options for the third item, and so on

There are $n \times (n-1) \times \ldots (n-k+1) = \frac{n!}{(n-k)!}$ ways of doing this.

Now, notice that picking 1 before 2 is the same as picking 2 before 1. So we have to count the number of ways in which we can pick k numbers, up to rearrangements. Since there are $k!$ ways to rearrange a bunch of k items, our final answer is

$$\binom{n}{k} = \frac{n!}{k!(n-k)!}$$

Tips on counting problems

1. Be careful about over-counting.

2. Be careful with whether you need the Addition or Product rule.

3. Sometimes it's easier to count things that we don't want and subtract them from the total.

Binomial theorem

For any positive integer n, we have

$$(x+y)^n = \binom{n}{0}x^n + \binom{n}{1}x^{n-1}y + \cdots + \binom{n}{n-1}xy^{n-1} + \binom{n}{n} = y^n$$

How do we show this? Write $(x+y)^n = (x+y)(x+y)\ldots(x+y)$. Now when we expand the right-hand side, the number of times $x^k y^{n-k}$ appears is the number of ways to choose k x's from those n x's, and choosing the remaining $n-k$ y's.

So the coefficient of $x^k y^{n-k}$ in the binomial expansion is $\binom{n}{k}$.

Some properties of the binomial coefficients

For any positive integer n and k, we have:

- $\binom{n}{0} = 1, \binom{n}{1} = n, \binom{n}{2} = \frac{n(n-1)}{2}$
- $\binom{n}{k} = \binom{n}{n-k}$
- $\binom{n}{k} + \binom{n}{k+1} = \binom{n+1}{k+1}$
- $\binom{n}{0} + \binom{n}{1} + \cdots + \binom{n}{n} = 2^n$

Example 13.1 (MAT 2014 Question 1.G). Let n be a positive integer. What is the coefficient of $x^3 y^5$ in the expansion of $(1 + xy + y^2)^n$

Solution. We have, $x^3 y^5 = (xy)^3 y^2$.

Recall how we expanded the expression $(x+y)^n$. When we expand $(1+xy+y^2)(1+xy+y^2)\ldots$, we want to count the number of ways to pick three xy, one y^2 and rest of the $1's$ from the n terms.

So we pick 3 xy's from n terms, that gives us $\binom{n}{3}$ ways.

Then we pick one y^2 from the remaining $n-3$ terms. Which is done in $n-3$ ways.

In total we have

$$\binom{n}{3}(n-3) = 4\binom{n}{4}$$

ways to get $x^3 y^5$ in the expansion. So the coefficient is $4\binom{n}{4}$ □

13.2 Probability

Definition

We also know if we toss a fair coin, where each side is equally like to come up, the probability that it will land on a head is $\frac{1}{2}$. Likewise, the probability of it landing on a tail is $\frac{1}{2}$ as well.

If we toss two coins, the outcome will be one of HH, HT, TH, TT. So the probability of seeing two heads is $\frac{1}{4}$.

Likewise, if there are n events, each equally likely of occurring, then the probability of any of the events happening is $\frac{1}{n}$. So, if you roll a fair dice, the probability that it will come up a 1 is $\frac{1}{6}$, because each six side has an equal probability of coming up.

Now, consider the event of getting an even number in the dice. There are three possible ways of this happening, that is, 2, 4 or 6 might come up. Now, each of these individual events has a probability of $\frac{1}{6}$. But the probability of any of them happening is $3 \times \frac{1}{6} = \frac{1}{2}$.

Likewise, if an event A can happen in m ways, and there are n possible outcomes, then the probability that A will happen is $\frac{m}{n}$. Formally, we write this as

$$\mathbb{P}(A) = \frac{m}{n}$$

and read it as, "the probability of A occurring is $\frac{m}{n}$".

> **Example 13.2** (AMC 1970 Problem 31). If a number is selected at random from the set of all five-digit numbers in which the sum of the digits is equal to 43, what is the probability that the number will be divisible by 11?

Solution. The maximum sum of 5 decimal digits is 45. So to have a five digit number with digit sum 43 we should have either one 7 or two 8.

Now, there are 5 integers of the first kind, with one 7,

$$79999, 97999, 99799, 99979, 99997$$

and 10 integers of the second kind, with two 8s

$$88999, 89899, 89989, 89998, 98899, 98989, 98998, 99889, 99898, 99988$$

Now, we test which of these numbers are divisible by 11. We get that only $99979, 97999$ and 98989 satisfy this property.

Hence, out of the total of 15 numbers 3 are divisible by 11. The probability of this event is $\frac{3}{15} = \frac{1}{5}$. □

Independence

Suppose we're rolling a dice and tossing a coin at the same time. What's the probability of a 6 coming up on the dice and the coin landing on a head?

The answer is $\frac{1}{6} \times \frac{1}{2} = \frac{1}{12}$. Why? Because the dice roll and the coin are **independent**, that is, the outcome of the roll of the dice does not effect the outcome of the coin toss, and vice versa.

If A and B are two events, then the event that A and B both happens is written in the set theoretic term: $A \cap B$. Now, if A and B are independent, then we have

$$\mathbb{P}(A \cap B) = \mathbb{P}(A) \times \mathbb{P}(B)$$

Now, consider a single dice roll. What's the probability that the number that comes up is an even number and less than or equal to 3?

The event that the number is even has a probability of $\frac{1}{2}$ and the event that it is less than or equal to 3 is $\frac{3}{6} = \frac{1}{2}$. But, both of these events can happen simultaneously only if the number that comes up is 2. That means, the probability of both of these events occurring at the same time is $\frac{1}{6}$. Note that, $\frac{1}{6} \neq \frac{1}{2} \times \frac{1}{2}$.

If two events, A and B are such, that, $\mathbb{P}(A \cap B) \neq \mathbb{P}(A)\mathbb{P}(B)$, then we say A and B are **dependent**. That is, the outcome of A effects the outcome of B in some way. In the previous example, the number being even and the number being less than 3 are not independent, because if one of them happens, then the outcome directly effects the outcome of the other event.

Mutually exclusive events

Consider the two events: A, a coin lands on its head, and B, it lands on its tail. These two events can't happen at the same time, and so they are mutually exclusive. Now, what's the probability that either of these events happen? It is $\frac{1}{2} + \frac{1}{2}$.

Suppose A and B are mutually exclusive events: both of them can't happen at the same time. If a is the number of ways A can happen, b is the number of ways B can happen, and if n is the total number of events, then, $\mathbb{P}(A) = \frac{a}{n}, \mathbb{P}(B) = \frac{b}{n}$. And, A or B can happen in $a+b$ ways, which gives,

$$\mathbb{P}(A \cup B) = \mathbb{P}(A) + \mathbb{P}(B)$$

13.2. PROBABILITY

where $A \cup B$ means either A or B happens.

Now, if A and B are not mutually exclusive, then three things can happen:

1. only A happens, and not B
2. only B happens, and not A
3. both A and B happens

Suppose there are a total of n events. If A can happen in a ways, B in b ways, and A, B both happens in c ways, then

$$\mathbb{P}(A) = \frac{a}{n}, \ \mathbb{P}(B) = \frac{b}{n}, \ \mathbb{P}(A \cap B) = \frac{c}{n}$$

Now, the probability that A or B occurs is = (the number of ways only A can happen) + (the number of ways only B can happen) + (the number of ways both A and B can happen). Note that, this is equal to $(a-c)+(b-c)+c$. That is, either A or B can happen in $a+b-c$ ways. So

$$\mathbb{P}(A \cup B) = \mathbb{P}(A) + \mathbb{P}(B) - \mathbb{P}(A \cap B)$$

Conditional probability

Let's go back to dice rolling. What's the probability that the number that comes up is even, given that the number is less than or equal to 3?

This is called conditional probability. We are asking, what's the probability that event A happens, given that the event B happens? That is, the probability of A conditioned to B. We write this probability as $\mathbb{P}(A|B)$.

In our case, if the number if less than or equal to 3, then we know that there can only be 3 possible outcomes: $1, 2, 3$, and only one of them is even. So the probability that the number is even given that it is less than or equal to 3 is $\frac{1}{3}$. Note that this is not equal to the $\frac{1}{6}$ probability of these two events occurring at the same time.

The formula for $\mathbb{P}(A|B)$ is given by,

$$\mathbb{P}(A|B) = \frac{\mathbb{P}(A \cap B)}{\mathbb{P}(B)}$$

when $\mathbb{P}(B) \neq 0$. If $\mathbb{P}(B) = 0$, that is, B can never happen, then $\mathbb{P}(A|B) = 0$ as well.

Example 13.3. You toss a fair coin three times. Given that you observe at least one head, what's the probability that you observe at least two heads?

Solution. Let A be the event that we observe at least two heads, and B be the event that we observe at least one head. So we are looking for $\mathbb{P}(A|B)$. We use the formula above.

First, let's find $\mathbb{P}(B)$. Only the case TTT is where we don't observe any head. We observe at least one head in all other 7 cases, so $\mathbb{P}(B) = \frac{7}{8}$.

Now, $A \cap B$ means we observe at least two heads. The four cases: TTT, HTT, THT, TTH are where we don't observe two heads. In all other 4 outcomes we observe at least two heads. So $\mathbb{P}(A \cap B) = \frac{1}{2}$.

Hence,

$$\mathbb{P}(A|B) = \frac{\mathbb{P}(A \cap B)}{\mathbb{P}(B)} = \frac{\frac{1}{2}}{\frac{7}{8}} = \frac{4}{7}$$

□

Random variables

A random variable is a numerical description of an outcome of a random event. For example, the event that coin lands on a head doesn't itself have a value. But once we say that head means 0 and tail means 1, then we can ask questions like, if we toss two coins and sum up their numerical values, what's the probability that the sum is 1?

In this case, the sum of two coin tosses to be one can happen only when one of the coins lands on head and the other lands on tail, meaning a $\frac{1}{2}$ probability (the desired outcomes are HT, TH).

A random variable X is a function from the set of events to the set of real numbers. If A is an event, then $X(A)$ is the value we assign to the event A.

For example, in the case of dice roll, if we assign the value $n = 1, 2, \ldots 6$ to the event of that n comes up on the roll, we have that

$$X(\text{event that 6 comes up}) = 6$$

We write the probability that the random variable X is equal to x as

$$\mathbb{P}(X = x) = \mathbb{P}(\text{any of the events } A \text{ happens, for which } X(A) = x)$$

Example 13.4. If we roll two dices, what's the probability that the sum of the two values that come up is (a) 1, (b) 2, (c) 7?

Solution. Note that the two numbers on the two dices are both greater or equal to 1. That means, the sum can never be 1. So the probability of this happening is 0.

Now, let X be the random variable representing this sum. That is

$$X(1 \text{ comes up on one dice, 2 comes up on the other}) = 3$$

and

$$X(4 \text{ comes up on one, 5 on the other}) = 9$$

Then the only way

$$X = 2$$

is when both dices show 1. That is, there's a $\frac{1}{6} \times \frac{1}{6}$ chance this happens.

For $X = 7$ to happen, one of the 6 events need to happen:

1. 1 comes on the first dice, 6 on the second
2. 2 on the first, 5 on the second
   ⋮
3. 6 on the first, 1 on the second

That means, out of the 36 outcomes of the event, 6 of them are our desired outcomes. That means $\mathbb{P}(X = 7) = \frac{6}{36} = \frac{1}{6}$. □

13.3 Walkthrough: MAT 2010 Question 7

Question

> In a game of Cat and Mouse, a cat starts at position 0, a mouse starts at position m and the mouse's hole is at position h. Here m and h are integers with $0 < m < h$.
>
> By way of example, a starting position is shown below where $m = 7$ and $h = 12$.
>
>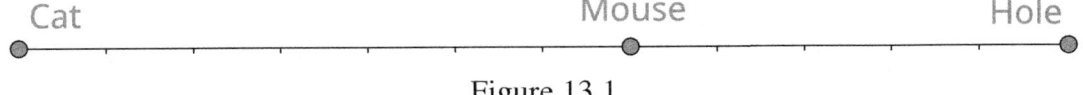
>
> Figure 13.1
>
> With each turn of the game, the mouse or cat (but not both) advances one position towards the hole on the condition that **the cat is always strictly behind the mouse and never catches it**. The game ends when the **mouse reaches the safety of its hole** at

position h.

This question is about calculating the number, $g(h,m)$, of different sequences of moves that make a game of Cat and Mouse.

Let C denote a move of the cat and M denote a move of the mouse. Then, for example, $g(3,1) = 2$ as MM and MCM are the only possible games.

Also $CMCCM$ is not a valid game when $h = 4$ and $m = 2$ as the mouse would be caught on the fourth turn.

Part i. Write down the five valid games when $h = 4$ and $m = 2$.

Part ii. Explain why $g(h, h-1) = h-1$ for $h \geqslant 2$.

Part iii. Explain why $g(h, 2) = g(h, 1)$ for $h \geqslant 3$.

Part iv. By considering the possible first moves of a game, explain why

$$g(h,m) = g(h, m+1) + g(h-1, m-1)$$

when $1 < m < h-1$.

Solution

(Part i) Write down the five valid games when $h = 4$ and $m = 2$.

Solution. There can be only two M's. We can try out all the cases by hand: MM, MCM, MCCM, CMM, CMCM. □

(Part ii) Explain why $g(h, h-1) = h-1$ for $h \geqslant 2$.

Solution. When $m = h-1$ then the mouse is only one stop away from its hole and the game will end with a single command M.

Also, before the mouse moves, the cat can move at most up to position $h-2$.

Hence the possible games are $M, CM, C^2M, C^3M, \ldots, C^{h-2}M$ making $h-1$ games in all. □

(Part iii) Explain why $g(h, 2) = g(h, 1)$ for $h \geqslant 3$.

Solution. If $m = 1$ then the first move must be made by the mouse. Otherwise the cat would

13.3. WALKTHROUGH: MAT 2010 QUESTION 7

catch it. Once the mouse has moved to the second position the remainder of the game is identical to a game where $m = 2$.

So every game with $m = 1$ is of the form MG where G is a uniquely specified game with $m = 2$. Hence $g(h,2) = g(h,1)$. □

> (Part iv) By considering the possible first moves of a game, explain why
>
> $$g(h,m) = g(h,m+1) + g(h-1,m-1)$$
>
> when $1 < m < h-1$.

Solution. Either the cat or the mouse can make the first move, so there are two cases.

Suppose the game begins with M. Then the remainder of the game is played with the mouse starting at $m+1$. So if the game is MG, then G can play out in $g(h,m+1)$ different ways.

If the game begins with C, then the game is CH. As afterwards, the cat starts at 1 H, which is not a valid game, this game is not valid in the general sense.

But, if we shift the starting point one unit to the right, then in this perspective, the cat starts at 0, the mouse starts at $m-1$ and the hole is at $h-1$. So in this sense there are $g(h-1,m-1)$ ways H can play out.

As these are the only two cases, and every game starts with either C or M, we have

$$g(h,m) = g(h,m+1) + g(h-1,m-1)$$

□

Printed in Great Britain
by Amazon